Anonymous

The distinctive Doctrines and Usages of the general Bodies

Of the Evangelical Lutheran Church in the United States

Anonymous

The distinctive Doctrines and Usages of the general Bodies
Of the Evangelical Lutheran Church in the United States

ISBN/EAN: 9783337051990

Printed in Europe, USA, Canada, Australia, Japan

Cover: Foto ©ninafisch / pixelio.de

More available books at **www.hansebooks.com**

THE

DISTINCTIVE DOCTRINES AND USAGES

OF THE

GENERAL BODIES

OF THE

EVANGELICAL LUTHERAN CHURCH

IN THE

UNITED STATES.

PHILADELPHIA, PA.:
LUTHERAN PUBLICATION SOCIETY.

COPYRIGHT, 1893,

BY

THE LUTHERAN PUBLICATION SOCIETY.

INTRODUCTION.

THE Lutheran Board of Publication issues this Book in response to the suggestion of one of its lay members. A brief yet comprehensive statement of the distinctive doctrines and usages of the General Bodies of the Evangelical Lutheran Church in this country, it was thought, would furnish information that would be desired by many, but which was not accessible in a cheap and convenient form. These distinctive features are here presented by the able and eminent writers who represent their respective General Bodies. Each writer views these differences from his own doctrinal standpoint, and is alone responsible for his statements. The reader, however, will find valuable information concerning the history of the several General Lutheran Bodies, and the causes which have originated and which yet perpetuate their organic separation.

The several papers are arranged in the order of the date of the organization of each General Body.

1. Joint Synod of Ohio, organized 1818.
2. General Synod, organized 1820.
3. German Iowa Synod, organized 1854.
4. General Council, organized 1867.
5. Synodical Conference, organized 1872.
6. United Synod in the South, organized 1886.

CONTENTS.

        PAGE

1. THE JOINT SYNOD OF OHIO—
   By Rev. Prof. M. Loy, D. D. 5

2. THE GENERAL SYNOD—
   By Rev. Prof. M. Valentine, D. D., LL.D. 34

3. THE GERMAN IOWA SYNOD—
   By Rev. Prof. S. Fritschel, D. D. 62

4. THE GENERAL COUNCIL—
   By Rev. Prof. H. E. Jacobs, D. D., LL.D. 87

5. THE SYNODICAL CONFERENCE—
   By Rev. Prof. F. Pieper 119

6. THE UNITED SYNOD IN THE SOUTH—
   By Rev. E. T. Horn, D. D. 167

(iv)

THE JOINT SYNOD OF OHIO.

BY

REV. PROF. M. LOY D. D.

IN the early years of the present century a few self-denying Lutheran ministers, imbued with the true missionary spirit, crossed the Allegheny mountains to break the bread of life to their brethren scattered in the Western wilds. Feeling the need of mutual counsel and encouragement, the little company in 1812 formed a special Conference, which subsequently developed into the Evangelical Lutheran Synod of Ohio and Adjacent States. The members encountered many difficulties, but by the blessing of God upon their zealous labors their numbers increased and their work prospered. In course of time it was deemed necessary to divide the Synod into districts, of which there are now ten. These hold meetings annually, while every two years they all meet in joint convention. The whole body is usually called the Joint Synod of Ohio.

From the beginning, the pastors and congregations thus united were intent on preserving and propagating the pure Lutheran faith, as with their limited opportunities they were able to apprehend and maintain it, and many were their conflicts with men who endeavored to lead their people astray by teaching otherwise than God's word teaches. The Confessions of the Church were held in high esteem, and appeals to them were frequent, although it was not until 1847 that the symbolical books were formally declared to be the confessional basis of Synod, and all candidates for the ministry were required to subscribe to them. This position has been firmly maintained until the present hour, and in this all that is distinctive of the Joint Synod of Ohio and Other States has its root and its explanation. In pursuance of her settled purpose by the grace of her Lord to be found faithful to the pure gospel as He mercifully restored it to His people in the glorious Reformation of the sixteenth century, she will not be enticed or goaded into any position or movement by which the saving truth set forth in the Confessions of the Evangelical Lutheran Church is compromised.

In taking this ground it never entered the minds of our pastors or people to place the Confessions of the Church on an equality with the Holy Scriptures. These are the very word of God in matter and in form. "All Scripture is given by inspiration of God, and is profitable for doctrine, for reproof, for correction, for instruction in righteousness, that the man of God may be perfect, thoroughly furnished unto all good works." 2 Tim.

iii. 16, 17. In the Scriptures the sovereign Lord of all has revealed His righteous and His gracious will in His own words. They are the only source of our knowledge of saving truth, and the only ultimate rule of faith and life. Their decision is final, and from them no appeal can be allowed. The symbols occupy a different place and serve a different purpose. They are not inspired writings. They set forth the faith which men have derived from the Holy Scriptures as the infallible source of saving truth. The Lutheran Church believes and therefore speaks. A doctrine does not become divine by her act of confessing it, and no one is bound to believe it because she confesses it. She confesses it because on the authority of God's word she believes it, and she asks others to believe it, and then with her to confess it, because the Scriptures teach it. We have the rule "that the word of God should frame articles of faith, otherwise no one, not even an angel." (*Smalc. Art.*, II., 2, 15.) From that rule we can under no circumstances depart, because under no circumstances could we consent to the subject's usurpation of authority which belongs only to the Sovereign. Such usurpation is a mark of the Antichrist, whose abominations the Reformation has taught us to shun as an offense against God and man. Our Confessions claim no authority over the souls of men, but simply declare the faith which lives in our souls and which clings to the word of the living God.

"He is the Lord; that is His name; and His glory will He not give to another." But when He speaks His people hear; and when they hear the good tidings which are for all people, how can they otherwise than publish them and bear witness to them for the glory of their Saviour and the good of their fellow-men? Those who have not the faith which the Lutheran Church confesses are not expected to confess it; but she believes, and therefore speaks.

In the nature of things this could not be without effect in her church life and practice. By the grace of God the Christians united in the Evangelical Lutheran Church have known and believed the Evangelical truth which is set forth in their confession; and on that basis her congregations are organized, her ministry is called, and her discipline is administered. It is this faith that gives her the distinctive character by which she is known as the Evangelical Lutheran Church. If some are not prepared to accept her confessions and enter into fellowship with her on these terms, they are manifestly not prepared to enter into fellowship with her at all. From the beginning she recognized no other terms, and could recognize no other without abandoning her faith and, with it, her life as the Evangelical Church of the Reformation. She came into being as a visible organization by confessing the truth of the Gospel which God in mercy restored to His people through the instrumentality of His chosen servant, and she continues in being by maintaining that blessed truth as the basis upon which her membership stands united.

The Joint Synod of Ohio recognizes the fact that the Evangelical Lutheran Church had her settled faith and her distinctive character when she witnessed her good confession at Augsburg in 1530, as she had declared it before in the universally accepted catechisms prepared by Dr. Luther. Those who sincerely adopt these confessions as the expression of their faith are in accord with her. Of pastors and teachers it is required indeed that they accept the entire Concordia of 1580. But this is only because a more thorough and a more extensive knowledge of revealed truth is expected of those who are called to teach it, not because agreement in the faith as set forth in the Catechism and the Augustana is insufficient for the unity of the Church. What we are concerned about is the faith once delivered to the saints, which we are in conscience bound to hold fast and perpetuate, and which is the same in all our symbols. Our controversy with those who reject a portion of them has its ground in the conviction that such rejection betrays a dissent from the Evangelical doctrine set forth in the Augsburg Confession, whose true import and meaning the later symbols develop and defend.

"Unto the true unity of the Church it is sufficient to agree concerning the doctrines of the Gospel and the administration of the Sacraments. Nor is it necessary that human traditions, rites, or ceremonies instituted by men should be alike everywhere: as St. Paul says, 'One faith, one baptism, one God and Father of all.' Eph iv. 5, 6." (*Augsburg Confession*, Art. VII.). That is the principle to which the Joint Synod is pledged, and by which her practice is governed. She loves the old ways of our fathers, and the beautiful forms in which they worshiped the Lord. She recognizes the benefits of uniformity in the ceremonies and usages of the churches, and heartily seeks to promote it. She desires, even in externals, to walk in the old paths and manifest her historical connection with the old Church. But she never fails to distinguish between that which is necessary and that which is free. What the Lord has not required, the servant of the Lord has no right to require as a condition of membership in His Church. He alone is Master, all we are brethren, who have no authority to impose and no obligation to bear any yoke of bondage. Diversity in matters merely human does not interfere with the unity of the Church, because the Lord Himself has given His people liberty to arrange them as in the varying circumstances of congregations they think best. Ceremonies instituted by men form no part of the service of God, and can never be of divine obligation. "We believe, teach and confess that the Church of God of every place and every time has the power, according to its circumstances, to change such ceremonies in such manner as may be most useful and edifying to the Church of God; nevertheless, that herein all inconsiderateness and offense should be avoided, and especial care should be taken to exercise forbearance to the weak in faith: 1 Cor. viii. 9; Rom. xiv. 13." (*Form. Conc.* Part I. ch. x. 4, 5.) Human ordinances are not divine laws. But when the Lord speaks all alike must bow to His authority. What He requires is necessary. From His Word there can be no appeal to human thoughts of expediency and human tastes and preferences. In what He teaches and requires there must be agreement among His disciples. And those who are called Lutherans have heard His voice, have believed His Word, and according to His will have confessed their faith in their symbols. Their Confession is the expression of their agreement concerning the doctrine of the Gospel. It contains only what is necessary "unto the true unity of the Church." On this ground they have united, and only on this ground can others unite with them.

The Joint Synod of Ohio, assured that the Evangelical Lutheran Confession sets forth the pure faith of the Gospel, diligently teaches it as well as confesses it with the Church of the glorious times of the Reformation, and earnestly maintains the necessity of its acceptance as a condition of reception into her congregations and communion at her altars. She does not grow weary of plying the Catechism and inculcating the precious truth unto salvation which it declares in a form as simple as it is profound in contents. She teaches her catechumens to know the Saviour, to confess Him before the world, and to walk worthy of Him who has purchased them with His blood, and called them into His kingdom. She is glad to number them among her communicants when they are ready to make the requisite confession and promise, but not until, by the blessing of God, this end has been accomplished. As the Church is the congregation of believers, she spares no effort to lead those committed to her instruction to an explicit faith before she leads them to a public confession. She insists on agreement concerning the doctrine of the Gospel in all cases as a condition of fellowship in the Holy Supper, and therefore insists upon the acceptance of the Lutheran Confession. She does this, not because she presumes that every particular visible Church has a divine right to organize on any basis that may be agreed on by the persons concerned, and then to insist on the acceptance of this basis as a condition of membership, simply because these are the original terms of the compact. That would be true of a society that is purely human and pretends to be nothing else. But it is not true of the Christian Church, which is not an association of men for purposes which they have chosen and with means which they have devised according to their own wisdom or pleasure. Men may form societies and lay down their own terms of admission and membership as they think best. But there is no such right to do what men please in the kingdom of Christ. In that He is Lord, and only those who are subject to Him as He speaks in His Word are entitled to a place in it. To be a congregation of believers the members must accept the faith declared in the Gospel, and in order to have unity they must agree in that faith. "Then said Jesus to those Jews which believed on Him, If ye continue in my word, then are ye my disciples, indeed; and ye shall know the truth, and the truth shall make you free." John viii. 31, 32. "Now, therefore, ye are no more strangers and foreigners, but fellow citizens with the saints, and of the household of God, and are built upon the foundations of the apostles and prophets, Jesus Christ Himself being the chief corner stone; in whom all the building fitly framed together groweth unto an holy temple in the Lord." Eph. ii. 19–21. Those who believe in the Saviour are His disciples, and they confess His name, declare His truth, and show forth His praise. The righteousness which is of faith speaketh on this wise, "The Word is nigh thee, even in thy mouth and in thy heart; that is, the Word of faith which we preach; that if thou shalt confess with thy mouth the Lord Jesus, and shalt believe in thy heart that God hath raised Him from the dead, thou shalt be saved. For with the heart man believeth unto righteousness, and with the mouth confession is made unto salvation." Rom. x. 8-10. By this confession Christians know each other as disciples of the same Lord, and on the ground of this they join together for the accomplishment of His gracious will. These confessing believers are exhorted to "keep the unity of the Spirit in the bond of peace." "Now I beseech you, brethren, by the name of our Lord Jesus Christ, that ye all speak the same thing, and that there be no divisions among you; but that ye be perfectly joined together in the same mind and in the same judgment." 1 Cor. i. 10. Christians are such because they believe in the heavenly truth which is revealed for our salvation. That is the one thing needful in church organization. Holding and confessing this, they may, in the exercise of their liberty, arrange as they deem expedient what the Master has not ordained, but left to their own wisdom. Congregations, as visible associations, may make their own regulations in regard to matters of indifference, but they are Christian congregations in virtue of their Christian faith and its confession, not in virtue of their human regulations. There can be no legitimate basis of union in the Church but that which the Lord lays down, and there can be no necessary conditions of membership and fellowship in the Church but those which the Lord prescribes.

The question of union, as the Joint Synod of Ohio sees it, is not one of mere expediency and courtesy. We cannot admit that the Evangelical Lutheran Church erred in her creed, and that from the start she sinned by uniting on that foundation and declining to unite with such as professed a different faith. She was not guilty of making needless divisions by her evangelical confession. She insisted only on the truth which the Scriptures teach and required only what the Lord requires as conditions of membership. She cannot alter these conditions now, because they are not of her making, and are not subject to her wisdom or her pleasure. They are obligatory upon her and upon all men by the authority of Him who is King in Zion. For this reason we are constrained to stand aloof from all church unions founded on any other basis than that of the truth revealed in God's Word and confessed in our symbols, and from all movements and demonstrations of a unionistic character, participating in which would imply the admission that the distinctive doctrines of the Evangelical Lutheran Church are no part of the faith once delivered to the saints, but are merely human opinions, and therefore have no divine right in Christendom. We heartily desire the union of Christians and of churches, but can see neither fidelity nor expediency in a pretense of union where there is no agreement concerning the doctrine of the gospel and the administration of the sacraments. The only Scriptural way to labor for union is to labor for unity in the faith and agreement in its confession. That is divinely required and therefore essential.

It is this that has prevented our organic connection even with other bodies that bear the Lutheran name. Of right this name stands for the historic Church of the Reformation with its incomparable Augsburg Confession. But unhappily not all who adopt the name adopt also that which it implies. Hence it comes that the Joint Synod of Ohio stands alone, notwithstanding that general Lutheran organizations have been formed around her, and notwithstanding her earnest desire that there should be no divisions among us.

There have been, and there still are, some who accept the Augsburg Confession as their own, but who were not and are not willing to declare the faith which it sets forth to be truly and really the one faith of the gospel, which God would have all men to receive, and agreement in which is necessary unto the true unity of the Church. In their own convictions they are in accord with the doctrines there confessed, or at least find no other confession that seems to them a more adequate expression of their beliefs. Many of them love the Lutheran name and its historic associations. But even those among them who defend the distinctive doctrines of our Confession usually regard them as opinions which at most have equal rights with the opinions proclaimed by other denominations, rather than as the truth of God which must be held fast at all hazards and at every cost, because this is the Master's will. In the exercise of what they deem charity, they therefore overlook the requirements of faith. The prevailing spirit among them has accordingly always been that of accommodation to the beliefs and practices of churches that have gained the ascendency among the American people. Some have even allowed themselves to be largely governed by the thought that what the great mass of professed Christians around them believe and do must be true and right, and that the creed and practice of the Lutheran Church should be shaped accordingly, as if she lived and could live only by their sufferance. Therefore evasive formulas were resorted to in adopting the Confession, and servile concessions were made to popular churches which are not in sympathy with the faith and spirit of the Church of the Reformation. The Joint Synod of Ohio, sincere in her confession of the old faith, could not and can not, by word or act, accept the consent of other denominations as the test of gospel truth, and could not and can not form an organic union with a body in which, notwithstanding the Lutheran name, men could make open assaults upon the doctrines confessed in the Catechism and Augsburg Confession without any fear of being called to account and subjected to discipline. These doctrines are taught in God's Word, and agreement concerning them is necessary unto the true unity of the Church, though thousands of professing Christians think proper to dispute them, and think themselves justifiable in setting forth a different creed and organizing churches on a different basis.

Even the formal acceptance of the Lutheran Confession may leave room for legitimate doubt whether the agreement exists which is necessary for union. Circumstances may be such as to force upon us the inquiry, whether such professed acceptance is meant as implying that Romanist and Reformed parties, secretists and chiliasts, shall not be admitted to our altars and churches. Important differences in this regard between us and others were brought to view in the controversy respecting the so-called "four points."

Convinced from their own publications of the Antichristian character and tendency of such associations, the Joint Synod of Ohio declares: "The rule among us must be, and ever remain, that members of secret societies cannot be received as members of our congregations, nor may they continue their membership or be admitted to the Holy Supper an indefinite length of time." The ground of this rule is not merely the appearance of evil that lies in their shunning the light, although the element of secresy is on this ground a serious objection. It awakens just suspicion, to which a Christian should not willingly make himself subject. But the evil is of a more dire and dangerous nature. When a society, such as that of the Free Masons, Odd Fellows, and those of similar character, inculcates rationalistic principles subversive of Christianity, destroying souls by leading them to trust in another righteousness than that of Christ, and to engage in another worship than that of the triune God, while at the same time it abuses the sacred oath and teaches and practices a so-called charity that is not in harmony with the gospel, we cannot regard its adherents, whatever their professions or their intentions may be, as in a proper condition for membership in the Christian Church and communion at her altar. They may not all be aware that their societies operate against the truth in Jesus, as many persons are not aware that in their natural state they are children of wrath, and without Christ can do nothing. But this does not change the fact. And it is the Church's calling to teach: where sin is not seen she must expose it, and where the saving truth is not known she must impart it. This our pastors are willing to do with all patience and with all allowance for circumstances; but they are not willing first to receive secretists into church fellowship and afterwards endeavor to do the work necessary to qualify them for it. While all secret societies are not in the same degree in conflict with Christian faith and love, and a difference will therefore be made in dealing with them, they are all objectionable, and the watchman on Zion's walls must warn against them and seek to rescue souls from their evil influence. With those who are willing to do nothing against these antichristian powers, and say nothing while souls committed to their charge are led to ruin by secretism, we are not agreed.

As regards chiliasm, the doctrine that Christ shall return to reign a thousand years upon earth prior to the final judgment, the Lutheran confessors at Augsburg in 1530 declared, that "they condemn others also who now scatter Jewish opinions, that before the resurrection of the dead the godly shall occupy the kingdom of the world, the wicked being everywhere suppressed." (*Augsb. Conf.*, Art. XVII.) The kingdom of our Lord is not of this world, but is a kingdom of grace in which believers are prepared for the kingdom of glory. According to the Apostles' Creed, which our children learn and confess before they are admitted to holy communion, Christ shall come at the last day, as the Scriptures teach, "to judge the quick and the dead," not to establish a temporal kingdom which would be essentially different from that which is already established, and in which He reigns by His word and sacraments as His blessed means of grace unto salvation. This is still the voice of the Evangelical Lutheran Church, and with this we are in complete and hearty accord. We ask only that earnest account be made of the truth confessed, and that accordingly no doctrine be sanctioned, not even by the consent implied in silence, which conflicts with that confession.

In the eyes of the Joint Synod, admitting ministers of other churches and of a different confession to our pulpits is inconsistent with her profession and her duty. Notwithstanding all the abuse heaped upon us for entertaining this conviction, we must persist in holding it and ordering our practice accordingly. Both faith and charity require it. We do not teach that ministers of other churches have no valid call to preach the Word and administer the sacraments, or that their ministrations are without efficacy. Nothing of that sort is taught in the Scriptures, and nothing of that sort appears in our Confessions. The Lord requires that ministers be rightly called by the Church, to which He has entrusted the means of grace, but does not command the rite of ordination to make the call valid, and least of all does He make the efficacy of the Word and sacrament dependent on ecclesiastical rites. As far as any hindrances arising from such questions are concerned, pastors of other churches would be cheerfully welcomed to our pulpits. But the Lutheran Church would betray the insincerity of her confession if she permitted men to teach in her congregations who do not even profess to believe her doctrines, and who, as regards the distinctive articles of her faith, avow their dissent from her teaching. Fully assured that what she confesses is the truth, which God requires her to teach for the glory of His name and the salvation of souls purchased by His blood, she cannot entrust the work of teaching in her churches and schools to men who do not agree with her concerning the doctrine of the gospel which she publicly proclaims in her symbols. Even if preachers of other denominations would, in order to gain access to our pulpits, give satisfactory assurances that they will teach nothing at variance with our faith, they could not, as long as they declare their adherence to a different confession, be permitted to preach to our congregations. That act of pulpit fellowship itself would be understood as a declaration on our part that the differences between their churches and ours are not of such a nature as to necessitate separate organizations, and therefore as an admission that we are maintaining divisions which have no ground in faith and conscience, and for that reason are sinful. The Lutheran Church is sincere in her confession, and therefore cannot consent, by any voluntary act of hers, to make the impression that in her estimation her distinctive doctrines are not of God and are not necessary unto the true unity of the Church. Her rule is, "Mark them which cause divisions and offenses contrary to the doctrine which ye have learned, and avoid them." Rom. xvi. 17. Those who believe what is written by inspiration of God for their learning, and from their hearts confess what they believe because it is the very truth of God, will readily understand why no considerations of courtesy are permitted to move us in opposition to the requirements of faith.

The same rule applies to the other question of altar fellowship. Admitting members of other denominations to communion in our churches would be practically declaring that the differences between them and us do not pertain to the faith, but are mere matters of human opinion; that therefore the Lutheran Church has grievously erred in putting her distinctive doctrines into her Confession as a part of the Christian Creed; and that by asserting agreement in these, as well as in the other parts of her Confession, to be requisite to true unity, and therefore a necessary condition of membership and fellowship, she has made needless divisions in the Church. The Joint Synod sincerely accepts the Lutheran Confession, and therefore cannot do this. She cannot admit that the Lutheran Church sets forth human opinions as articles of faith, and thus seeks to bind human ordinances on the consciences of Christ's free people. In her eyes such an admission would undermine her confessional foundation and brand the great Church of the Reformation as an unevangelical sect, which before God has no right to live. Such doctrines as those taught in our Catechism and Augsburg Confession concerning Absolution, Baptism, and the Lord's Supper, for example, are not products of human reason, or opinions that rest on rational probabilities. They belong to our faith. We believe them because God's Word teaches them, and we confess them because we believe them. If others do not believe them, we deplore it and wish it were otherwise, but that cannot be allowed to shake or disturb our faith. Their conduct is not our rule or standard. We abide by the Holy Scriptures, whatever attitude others may assume towards the doctrines which they teach us. Meantime it does not enter our hearts to think or say that all other denominations are not churches, or that their members are not Christians. The imputation to us of such opinions is sheer uncharitableness. There is nothing to warrant and nothing to justify it. We hold no such opinions, and maintain nothing from which they could be justly inferred. There are churches that err. They are churches notwithstanding their errors, and they would not be churches if there were no Christian believers among them. But we could not answer for it on the judgment day if by word or act we gave our sanction to their error. Who shall blame us for leaving the responsibility for it to those who make divisions contrary to the doctrine which we have learned, and for abiding by the truth of the gospel, notwithstanding their obstinate persistence in error and consequent refusal to join us in confessing that truth? Erring denominations may still retain enough of the heavenly doctrine to lead souls to

Christ, the only and the all-sufficient Saviour of men, and may thus have the children of God among them who properly constitute the Church. But that does not render their errors harmless. On the contrary, these are a source of constant danger to the spiritual life of the individual and of the congregation. "Shun profane and vain babblings, for they will increase unto more ungodliness; and their word will eat as doth a canker." 2 Tim. ii. 16, 17. Error spreads; the little leaven permitted to work, in course of time leavens the whole lump. When the Church becomes indifferent to the purity of the faith, Satan uses his opportunity of banishing the truth revealed for our salvation and urging men to flee for refuge to their own natural resources which cannot save. The subject is one of such serious moment, involving the glory of our blessed Redeemer and the salvation of millions of our ruined race, that thoughtful minds and loving hearts must look with amazement upon the sad and strange spectacle of Christian men condemning the firm adherence of other Christian men to the saving truth which they have learned from the Scriptures, and for which, according to the divine command, they earnestly contend, even if such contention result in the separation of those who will not accept it. If some will not join us in confessing the truth, we certainly cannot join them in confessing their error. Neither can we admit such human error to be ultimately as good and as effectual for salvation as the good tidings revealed for our enlightenment from heaven. We cannot, in our loyalty to our Lord, do otherwise than decline to have fellowship at the altar of the Lord with those who teach and confess otherwise than the Word of God teaches. As to whether those who present themselves for communion are really Christians or not, that is, as to whether they believe in the Lord Jesus Christ unto the saving of the soul or not, that is altogether a different matter. It is well for all to bear in mind that under no circumstances is it man's calling or business to judge the heart. That is God's prerogative. If a person is not willing to accept the truth which the Church believes and confesses, we can only say that he is not yet prepared to meet the conditions of church fellowship. Of that the Church must judge, and nothing more. Our pastors are ready to teach the truth which by the grace of God she possesses. If any one will not accept instruction, or being instructed will not accept the doctrine of the gospel, agreement concerning which is necessary to the true unity of the Church, he must answer for it, as we must answer for our teaching and confession: God is his judge, as He is ours. In view of that judgment we cannot abandon our Scriptural faith and confession and make other terms of fellowship to suit his dissenting opinions.

The Joint Synod of Ohio has always been willing to make due allowance for hindrances put into the way of consistent Lutheran practice by customs handed down from times of relaxed vigilance. She is well aware that where unionism and secretism have held sway for years they cannot be eradicated in a day. She does not expect this. She advocates no rash and revolutionary measures. But with her Lutheran Confession she insists that agreement concerning the doctrine of the gospel is a necessary condition of union and communion in the Church; that the doctrine of the gospel, concerning which agreement is necessary, is set forth in her confession of faith; and that she could not be faithful if she admitted that in any case such agreement is not necessary. When the confessional principle is once accepted and the teaching is fully and faithfully conformed to it as the regulative of Church practice, she can patiently wait while the Word of God is doing its work in the congregations. She has had need for patience in her own congregations, and has need for patience still. But she can allow no exceptions to the rule that those who preach in her pulpits and commune at her altars must agree in the faith which the gospel teaches and which the Evangelical Lutheran Church confesses. There are individuals whose weakness demands great tenderness of treatment and whose previous training pleads for patience; there may be instances in which it is difficult to decide whether the necessary conditions of fellowship have been met, and which leave room for a difference of judgment in this regard; but these, like all other cases, must be treated under the rule that agreement concerning the doctrine of the gospel is necessary to the true unity of the Church, not as exceptions that justify a violation of the confessional principle.

To candid minds it must be apparent, that when a body claiming to be Lutheran finds an honest adherence to the Lutheran faith and confession, in doctrine and in practice, a valid ground for establishing opposition congregations on a professedly more liberal basis, to the great detriment of sound evangelical doctrine and discipline, their professions of agreement with us cannot be accepted with unquestioning confidence. Even when the Confessions of the Lutheran Church are formally adopted, there is still an essential disagreement between those who hold the doctrines there set forth to be the eternal truth of God, agreement in which is necessary to the true unity of the Church, and those who, while they profess to accept them, still regard them merely as the expression of human opinions which we have not even the right, much less the duty, to enforce in Church organization and discipline, and disagreement concerning which can, therefore, form no barrier to Church fellowship. If that which our Augsburg Confession publishes as the pure Christian faith is the very truth of the gospel, given by inspiration of God in the Scriptures for all men and all times, we can only insist on its maintenance, whether men, call themselves what they may, accept it and go with us, or reject it and turn away from us; if it be not the blessed truth revealed from heaven for our learning and the saving of our sinful souls, there can be no more grievouss sin than that of attempting to lay it as a yoke upon the necks of God's people, and making and maintaining divisions on account of it. The Lutheran Church believes the truth which God has made known to her by the gospel, and therefore cannot think of relinquishing it, or any part of it, for the accommodation of those who decline to believe it. That is the position of the Joint Synod.

On the subject of predestination, which has been much mooted in recent years, she maintains the same fidelity to the precious truth of the gospel. Practically the Lutheran Church has always been a unit in the rejection of those gloomy errors which center in the theory of absolute election to faith. While she never swerved from the fundamental truth that salvation is by grace alone, she just as firmly maintained the other fundamental truth that salvation is by faith alone, as the only means by which the soul can appropriate the merits of Christ. Nor was she ever moved by the reasoning of Reformed churches, plausible as it is sometimes made to appear, that if faith has any influence on the saving of the soul, man's power and merit must have some share in effecting the salvation. The plain teaching of the Bible, that all is due to God's grace, notwithstanding that faith is indispensable, proves such reasoning false. "For by grace are ye saved through faith; and that not of yourselves: it is the gift of God." Eph. ii. 8. "For God so loved the world that He gave His only begotten Son, that whosoever believeth in Him should not perish, but have everlasting life." John iii. 16. The Holy Spirit knows better than man in his pride of reason what is requisite that all may be ascribed to grace and all the glory may be given to God. Salvation is by grace alone, and all the glory of it belongs to God; and yet the rule is clearly revealed that "he that believeth shall be saved, but he that believeth not shall be damned." Faith is necessary to salvation. For human thought there is unquestionably a difficulty in the doctrine. If it depends wholly on God's will who shall be saved, it is not easy to see how, since the Scriptures declare that the will of God is the salvation of all, any soul should be lost; if it depends in any degree on man, it is not easy to see how, since the Scriptures declare that all are dead in trespasses and sins, any soul should be saved. To overcome the difficulty, Calvinists assume that God makes a difference by electing some and not electing others, by His sovereign right choosing some persons whom He pleases to save, and by His sovereign might accomplishing His pleasure in the chosen few, while all the others are passed by and left to perish in their helplessness. The dreadful solution satisfies the reason of many, though it may shock their hearts, and in these latter evil days even some of the Lutheran name have been induced to adopt it in its main features, arguing indeed that salvation is thus still by faith, because God always makes believers of those whom He elects to salvation, but overlooking the fact that in the same sense salvation is by good works, since He always leads His people heavenward in the paths of holiness. No reasoning could induce the Joint Synod of Ohio to turn away from the comforting truth of the gospel for which the Lutheran Church contended during the past centuries of her history, and to exchange it for Calvinistic errors which her teachers have again and again exposed and refuted from the Holy Scriptures.

But she does not on that account adopt the other solution which reason suggests of the problem. Salvation is by faith, but it is not by man's power and merit. Faith is the gift of God, but it is not forced upon any man; and it has no merit of its own, but appropriates Christ's merit. Salvation is all a work of God's grace, and all the praise belongs to Him. But when he calls men by the Gospel it is His will that not only an elect portion of the called, but that all should believe it and be saved, and He offers to all of them the grace needful to this end. If any to whom the Word of this salvation is sent are not saved, it is only because the will of God, which in the domain of grace never works irresistibly and never coerces the human will, was wilfully resisted. "How often would I," says our merciful Saviour, "have gathered thy children together, even as a hen gathereth her chickens under her wings, and ye would not." Matt. xxii. 37. "That, however," says our Confession, "many are called and few are chosen, does not mean that God is unwilling that all should be saved; but the reason is that they do not at all hear God's Word, but wilfully despise it, close their ears and harden their hearts, and in this way foreclose the ordinary way to the Holy Ghost, so that He cannot effect His work in them, or when it is heard, they consider it of no account and do not heed it." (*Form. Conc.* 526, 11). By this we abide. So far as the Joint Synod of Ohio is concerned, it is utterly vain to argue that after all our explanations there are still difficulties in our doctrine of conversion which would be escaped by adopting the Calvinistic system. It is vain, because she builds her faith on Holy Scripture, not on man's speculative ability or his success in solving theological or psychological problems. Whatever may be the explanation of the mystery encountered in the doctrine of human conversion by divine grace, we are quite sure that it is not to be found in the unscriptural assumption that with God there is respect of persons, and that He saves some because He wills it and elects them to faith and salvation, and does not save others because He had not the will to elect them. He would have all men to be saved and to come to a knowledge of the truth, and is "not willing that any should perish, but that all should come to repentance." 2 Pet. iii. 9. The responsibility of choosing death rather than life rests wholly upon the unbelieving sinner, in no respect and in no degree upon our blessed Lord, who left nothing undone that His grace could do to effect the salvation of all alike. The doctrine of an absolute election, in which no reference is had to the soul's relation to Christ by faith, solves difficulties only at the expense of gospel grace and truth and comfort, and in fidelity to Christ and the Church we can only reject it.

The Evangelical Lutheran Joint Synod of Ohio and Other States stands alone, not because she closes her eyes to the importance of uniting Synods and churches, and not because she has any special theological or ecclesiastical tendencies to maintain, or any peculiar phase of Lutheranism to advocate, but simply because she believes the sacred truth which the Evangelical Lutheran Church confesses, holds it to be the doctrine of the gospel concerning which agreement is necessary to the true unity of the Church, and can therefore unite with others on no other basis, hearing and heeding what the Spirit saith unto the churches: "Hold that fast which thou hast, that no man take thy crown."

THE GENERAL SYNOD.

BY

REV. PROF. M. VALENTINE, D. D., LL.D.

OCCASION OF ORGANIZATION.

THE General Synod was formed in 1820, in order to complete the organization of the Lutheran Church in the United States, uniting its different Synods in fellowship and work. Before that time there was no general body to exhibit its unity, or through which all parts could co-operate in common effort for its proper development and prosperity. Every denomination necessarily has certain interests and enterprises, such as Education, Home and Foreign Missions, and Church Extension, that can be properly and efficiently carried on only by concerted action and the help of the whole communion. At that period our Church in America reached the strength and wide territorial expansion that called for the advantages of such a general confederation. Then, and for these reasons and general purposes, the General Synod came into being. Some of these objects may not have been definitely and fully included in the design of the founders, but manifestly, as events soon showed, they were included in the eye and ordering of Providence. The General Synod thus arose in the normal and regular course of our Church's development and proper organization in this land.

The need of this completing step was clearly seen and deeply felt. There was no general organization in existence providing for the necessary union. One had to be created. The origin of the General Synod was thus not only legitimate, as arising in the natural and normal order of our Church's progress in our country, but demanded by the pressing work to which God was calling it. It exists, clearly, as a product of that divine Providence which was leading the Lutheran Church in the United States onward to complete organization and unity for its great spiritual mission and work. This feature of its origin is part of the General Synod's peculiar honor, and a fact that rightly exalts it in Christian regard. Its organization formed a great Providential epoch in the development and history of our Church in America.

Most fittingly, therefore, the Constitution of the body places these fundamental ideas at the very basis of its existence, as formed: "Relying upon God our Father, in the name of our Lord Jesus Christ, under the guidance and direction of the Holy Spirit in the Word of God, for the promotion of the practice of brotherly love, to the furtherance of Christian concord, to the firm establishment and continuance of the unity of the Spirit in the bond of peace, and for the accomplishment of the grand design for which the Church of Christ was established on earth." (Preamble.)

The first step to this organization was taken by the Synod of Pennsylvania, which at that time embraced the majority of the Lutheran churches and pastors in the United States. There were, however, four other Synods already formed, viz.: the Synod of New York, the Synod of Maryland and Virginia, the Synod of North Carolina, and the Synod of Ohio. The fellowship between these Synods had been limited to interchange of delegates and other casual intercommunication. At the meeting of the Pennsylvania Synod at Harrisburg, Pa., in 1819, it declared it to be "desirable that the different Evangelical Lutheran Synods in the United States should in some way or other stand in closer connection with each other," and appointed a committee to consider and prepare a feasible plan for such a union. In Baltimore, the next year, this committee reported a plan which, after careful discussion, was adopted, and submitted to the separate Synods. Upon the approval of the plan by them a convention was called and held in Hagerstown, Md., October 22, 1820, and the organization formally effected. The Synod of Ohio, however, failed to appear or unite with the organization.

GROWTH.

The growth of the General Synod, beginning with these four bodies, may be seen in the following statement, exhibiting, at intervals of ten years, the number of Synods, ministers, and communicant members belonging to it, viz:

Date.	Synods.	Ministers.	Communicants.
1820	4	100	
1830	3	76	14,118
1840	7	130	29,106
1850	16	364	63,401
1860	26	864	164,226
1870	21	647	98,077
1880	23	845	125,317
1890	24	1002	164,640

The decrease, as seen in this statement between 1860 and 1870, is explained by the separation of all the five Synods of the southern States, viz: of North Carolina, South Carolina, Virginia, Western Virginia, and Texas, in consequence of the civil war, and also by the withdrawal of the Pennsylvania Synod, the Synod of New York, the English Synod of Ohio, and a portion of the Pittsburgh Synod, which formed or afterward united with the General Council. When it is remembered that these withdrawals left less than half of its already attained church-membership, these figures will show that despite that immense loss, the General Synod has had a wonderfully rapid growth and prosperity.

GENERAL PRINCIPLES.

The general principles which controlled the form and constitution of the body were such as arose from the actual condition of the Church and the objects sought to be attained through the organization. These objects were, primarily, not doctrinal, but *practical*. It was wanted as a union for fellowship and earnest church work and enterprise. In it the Synods came together on the recognized and unquestioned fact that the bodies so uniting were Evangelical Lutheran bodies. The wise and godly founders were men of great spiritual earnestness, all aglow with intelligent zeal for the prosperity and extension of our American branch of the great Church of the Reformation. They were true sons of Issachar, understanding the times, and knowing what our Lutheran Israel ought to do, 1 Chron. xii. 32.

As the union was thus formed for fellowship in practical enterprise, in the way of united effort and labor for the upbuilding of the Church and the right accomplishment of its work, the character and powers of the organization were adjusted especially to this grand design. No worthier or nobler aim could have guided its founders. Yet, though not primarily meant for the settling of doctrinal questions or dogmatic views, the General Synod at once put a solid Lutheran basis under the practical work it undertook, as for instance, in the Constitution of the Theological Seminary

OF THE GENERAL SYNOD. 39

which it immediately proceeded to establish at Gettysburg. In this it enacted the law: "In this Seminary shall be taught, in the German and English languages, the fundamental doctrines of the Sacred Scriptures, as contained in the Augsburg Confession." Similar regard to the distinctive Lutheran system of theology was shown in the Constitution which it prepared for Synods. It began its practical work with this high emphasis on Lutheran doctrine. *It took the lead in establishing among us the proper authority of our Church's great Confession.*

DOCTRINAL BASIS.

The doctrinal basis of the General Synod is given in its Constitution, and in a resolution adopted in connection with the declaration of its confessional requirement.

The Constitution requires all Synods uniting with it to "*Receive and hold, with the Evangelical Lutheran Church of our fathers, the Word of God as contained in the canonical Scriptures of the Old and New Testaments, as the only infallible rule of faith and practice, and the Augsburg Confession as a correct exhibition of the fundamental doctrines of the divine Word, and of the faith of our Church as founded upon that Word.*" (Minutes of General Synod, 1864.)

The *resolution*, adopted at the same time, as an explanatory declaration upon a number of points on which the correctness of the Augsburg Confession had been called in question, is as follows:

"This General Synod, resting on the Word of God as the sole authority in matters of faith, on its infallible warrant rejects the Romish doctrine of the real presence or transubstantiation, and with it the doctrine of consubstantiation; rejects the Romish Mass and all the ceremonies distinctive of the Mass; denies any power in the sacraments as an *opus operatum*, or that the blessings of Baptism and the Lord's Supper can be received without faith; rejects auricular confession and priestly absolution; holds that there is no priesthood on earth but that of all believers, and that God only can forgive sins; and maintains the divine obligation of the Sabbath."

This explanation, as repudiating some errors that had been alleged to be in the Confession, and affirming its real sense, must be regarded as part of the General Synod's doctrinal position. It is not meant, however, as either taking anything away from the teaching of the Confession or adding anything to it.

The General Synod, it will be observed, grounds its doctrinal position in a twofold way. First and absolutely on "*the Word of God*" as contained in the holy Scriptures. This it takes as "*the only infallible rule of faith and practice*"—sole norm and final umpire. Secondly, on "*the Augsburg Confession.*" This it receives and adopts as "a *correct exhibition of the fundamental doctrines of the divine Word and of the faith of our Church as founded upon that Word."* The Augsburg Confession therefore, the adoption of which is required of Synods as conditional for entrance, becomes the statement of the doctrinal position and teaching of the General Synod. In harmony with this basis, it has also set forth Luther's Small Catechism as its handbook and guide in catechetical instruction.

THE AUGSBURG CONFESSION ONLY.

The General Synod does not include in its confessional basis any of the other writings that have been, to greater or less extent, accepted as doctrinal standards in some places, such as The Apology to the Augsburg Confession, Luther's Larger Catechism, the Smalkald Articles, and especially the Formula Concordiæ of 1580.

The reasons for not enforcing obligation to these are:

First, that the Augsburg Confession is *the only universal symbol of the Lutheran faith, the one standard that alone has marked and authenticated it always and everywhere.* It identifies the Lutheran Church the world over—"the Church of the Augsburg Confession." The doctrinal definitions and developments in the other writings, especially in the Formula Concordiæ, so far as they are not contained in the Augsburg Confession, are not essential to the Lutheran doctrinal system. They form "developments" which, in proportion to the stress laid on them, constitute *types* or *varieties* of Lutheran explanation, but not generic Lutheranism itself.

Secondly, these other symbols have never been necessary to constitute a Lutheran Church. A half-century of the existence of the Lutheran Church passed before the Formula Concordiæ was written, the symbol that is most strenuously advocated by some. And after it was written it was never universally received or made binding. It has always been more or less disowned, and a source of contention. The Lutheran Church has existed and done its grand work in whole countries without it, standing forth at the time and in history in unimpeachable and undiminished Lutheran rank and honor, as in Denmark, Sweden, Holstein, Pomerania, Anhalt, Hesse, the Palatinate of Zweibrücken, Brunswick, Nuremberg, and elsewhere. So also in many Lutheran cities. Those that did not adopt it could not be deprived of their Lutheran standing, but maintained their true Lutheran freedom upon the basis of the great fundamental Confession of Augsburg. Of our Church in Denmark at the present time, one of her clergymen has just now written: "As to the doctrine of the Danish Church, she accepts as her symbols, besides the three œcumenical symbols, the *Confessio Augustana invariata* [the unaltered Augsburg Confession] and Luther's Lesser Catechism. The other symbolical books of the Lutheran Churches do not concern us at all."*

Thirdly, *these additional symbols are not adapted to unite the whole Lutheran Church.* Their particular explanations and developments touching different views and tendencies that from the first and always have had place and advocacy in the Church, do not unite, but separate between those who agree upon the common basis of the Augsburg Confession, and would be one. The specific developments and extended definitions, pressing disputed points one-sidedly into narrowest particularity, or unnecessary prominence, have not worked unity or union, but organized parties and divisions. They can unify only fractions, greater or less, of the whole Church, in separation from other parts, as history clearly shows. How ill-adapted and inefficient a required adoption of the whole mass of these symbols is to unite the Church, is plain from the painful fact that the general bodies in this country actually adopting them have nevertheless been, and are, arrayed against each other, and refuse each other fellowship in pulpit and at altar.

Fourthly, in the adoption of the Augsburg Confession alone as its basis, the General Synod allows full liberty to persons within it to accept *for themselves* any or all of the special doctrinal views, even down to the minutest particulars, of the rest of the so-called symbols. Its mode and measure of con-

* Handbook of Lutheranism, p. 86.

fessional subscription excludes no one, as it oppresses no one. Nothing can exclude him, except his personal unwillingness to hold fellowship and co-operate in church work with brethren who fail to agree exactly with his own accepted explanation of each and every aspect of Lutheran teaching, making fellowship and co-operation dependent on being able, or allowed, to impose his own particular conceptions on all his brethren. The General Synod's basis is thus wisely and lovingly adapted to unite *all real Lutherans.* They are invited to stand and work together, in the use and concession of liberty, on the common ground of the Church's great system of doctrine. The only limitation of the liberty of those who believe and accept for themselves even every specification of the Form of Concord, is the disallowance of a sometimes assumed right of imposing their particularity or particularities upon the rest; or the use of the freedom and places of trust of the General Synod to abridge or subvert its liberal, generic, catholic basis and spirit, for a contracted and intolerant one. The exclusion of such intolerant temper and demand is essential at once to the General Synod's catholic basis itself, and to the permanence of its own existence.

JUSTICE AND SAFETY OF THIS BASIS.

On this basis the General Synod is secured on both sides. On the one side it is secured in *fidelity to the Lutheran system of doctrine;* on the other against the narrowness and wrong of obliging any real Lutherans to stand outside.

By the first, it is placed in the true and unquestionable succession of the historic Lutheran Church, with its positive and full maintenance of the saving doctrines of the gospel. For the Augsburg Confession is no "negative" exhibition of Christianity. It asks no one to breathe in a vacuum. It is a most positive and full assertion of the fundamental and saving doctrines of the divine word and of the faith of our Church as founded on that word; a generic but positive creed, well suited to be the universal symbol of the revived Christianity which Luther and his co-laborers meant to restore to the whole world. The General Synod is thus fully secured upon our Church's historic and safe foundations.

By the second security, it is guarded against the injustice of excluding any genuine Lutherans, though for themselves they may hold any or all the doctrinal specifications and developments found in the rest of the so-called symbols. It neither forces nor leaves any necessity for antagonistic Lutheran general organizations. The General Synod believes that unless there is an undue magnifying of merely incidental or unessential points, peculiar to some partisan contention, and with proper Christian and fraternal spirit, the whole Lutheran Church in our land can, as it ought to, unite and work together on the basis of our generic Lutheran Creed.

THE POSSIBILITY OF UNION.

It thus becomes clear that the General Synod, representing our Lutheran. Church in its true doctrines and full breadth and greatness, apart from any special type, offers the only hope of ever composing our strifes and ending our divisions. *On the common Confession of Augsburg all Lutherans agree.* It is vain to hope for unity or union in America on the restrictive basis upon which three centuries of effort have not given it in Europe. For those who demand the Form of Concord divide as to *its* teachings and implications and refuse each other fellowship. The Lutheranism of this country, a meeting place of the Lutherans from all lands, *ought* to be nothing smaller than the Lutheranism of the whole Church. The wisdom and necessity of the General Synod's basis, in this connection, cannot be better or more decisively expressed than in the words of Dr. Krauth, in 1857: "The Augsburg Confession is the symbol which alone has been recognized always, everywhere, and by all Lutherans, as their Confession; and as Lutheranism in America should rest on nothing that is local or national, but should embody only that which is common to the Lutheranism of all lands, it is a vital point she [the General Synod] should acknowledge as her creed that only whose reception in the Church has been universal. The Augsburg Confession is the symbol of Lutheran catholicity; all the other distinctive portions of the Book of Concord are symbols of Lutheran particularity, creeds of Lutheran Churches, but not in an undisputed sense of the Lutheran Church."

It is manifestly not necessary, therefore, nor even consistent, in this connection, to attempt to specify and set forth the precise Lutheran teaching of the General Synod, on the various topics in controversy in our Church; since it is of the very essence of its confessional position and claim that the Augsburg Confession is itself the statement of what it holds, and that in the differences of understanding and explanation that have always marked the interpretation of some of its statements, undisturbed liberty shall be enjoyed. In this its Lutheranism is both true in itself, and just to the whole great Lutheran Church of the Reformation and of history.

WORSHIP.

With respect to WORSHIP the General Synod is in harmony with the liturgical principles which from the first obtained in our Church. It looks upon a moderate, evangelical, spiritual Order of Service, properly connected with the best devotional usage of our past, as of great importance. But it holds, with the Augsburg Confession, Art. VII., that sameness or uniformity of ceremonies is not essential. A general uniformity is felt to be desirable, but not held to be necessary. According to the well-established Lutheran principle, asserted by Luther and set forth in early Lutheran Orders themselves, the use of particular forms of service is regarded as belonging, not to the sphere of law, but to the freedom of the congregations. This freedom the General Synod does not abridge, but defends. The Forms of Service set forth are not enforced, and may not be, by authority or constraint, and are to be used by the churches only as they are found to be to edification and conducive to the best spiritual life and work of the Church. Under this freedom, the principle of adaptation to new conditions and circumstances, followed in the earliest construction of Lutheran liturgies, is emphasized as still presenting both a right and a duty, in the altered conditions of our Church in this country. As long as congregations order their worship in harmony with the doctrines of the gospel, as set forth in the Augsburg Confession, their Lutheran standing is not disturbed by such adaptive modifications.

The General Synod has practically adjusted itself to these acknowledged principles of our Church on the subject of worship, and to her historic usage, seeking at once proper conformity to the moderate liturgical Orders of the past, and needful adaptation to the present conditions and necessities, and submitting Forms of Service for the free use of the congregations, as they may be found adapted to edification of the Christian life and the evangelization of the world.

DOCTRINE AND LIFE.

The revival of deep evangelical piety in Germany under the spiritual labors of Spener, Arndt, Francke, and their associates, which reached our country through the great and consecrated labors of the patriarch Muhlenberg and other godly ministers from Halle, gave its clear and strong impress to the religious life of the churches and Synods that formed the General Synod. That great and gracious quickening that had come as a renewal of formal orthodoxy to its true life, restored the heart again to its place in religion. Its grand import was that the pure doctrine is not to stand apart from daily life, but, under the power of the Holy Ghost, is to appear in a truly renewed, sanctified, and holy character. The truth is not to be "held in unrighteousness" of life. "Christ in us;" is to be emphasized as well as Christ "for us." To be a Christian means more than an assent to an orthodox creed and the outward formalities of sacraments and church-membership. True faith is to be understood as meaning, not a mere cold, unspiritual acceptance of the general and particular doctrines of Christianity, but especially a living appropriation by the believing *heart* (Rom. x: 10) of the Lord Jesus Christ in all his saving offices and sanctifying grace—such a vital faith as becomes, through the Holy Spirit in the Word, the power of a new and holy life in obedience and love. This connection of the General Synod, as inheriting, in the way mentioned, some of the best fruits of that great spiritual awakening, which thus restored the deep, earnest piety for which the Lutheran Reformation originally stood, has given to this body a clear and positive characteristic that has marked its whole history. The essential idea of that restorative movement—living piety along with orthodox belief—has remained vital in the General Synod. It is traceable in many aspects or features of common personal piety, of congregational order and custom, and of general church life. It is seen in the prevalent type of preaching, earnest, searching and practical, closely applying the truth as it is in Jesus to the state of the heart and the requirements of personal duty and Christian temper in all the relations of life and conduct. It has caused the ministers of the body to be the ever-pronounced foes of prevalent evils, and champions of every good cause. It has fostered mid-week devotional services, prayer-meetings, Sunday-schools, and Bible classes, and is ever ready to use every auxiliary, in harmony with the teaching of the Holy Scriptures, for the development of Christian activity and the doing of good. It has given to catechetical instruction a tender and faithful spirituality that makes this great agency for the conversion and salvation of the young most effectual for the precious objects for which catechisation has its prominent place among the usages of our Church. The General Synod has always stood for a living piety.

CATECHISATION.

The General Synod thoroughly adopts and exalts to its full place of prominence this custom of our Church, for the proper instruction of the young and their right preparation for admission to Communion. While not neglecting the solemn obligation, through faithful preaching of the gospel, to seek conversions from the world and bring in those that are without, it lays the utmost stress upon the duty of bringing up the young in the "nurture and admonition of the Lord," especially those to whom God, through holy baptism, has given the "adoption of children," that they may become, and truly be, in heart and life, all that is meant in their divinely-given church-membership. As "the force, value, and blessing of the baptismal covenant and grace are to extend through their whole subsequent lives," the method of their proper care and spiritual development is regarded as distinctly educational, under the regenerating and sanctifying power of the Holy Ghost through the truth as it is in Jesus Christ. And the General Synod seeks to gather thus into the catechetical class also the yet unbaptized children and adults from the world, and in this way bring them to true and living faith in Jesus Christ, and into the Church.

This catechisation, therefore, is not looked upon as a mere routine formality, or a process of simply intellectual indoctrination, that shall, *of course*, terminate in confirmation, irrespective of genuine faith, spiritual interest, or a purpose of true Christian obedience on the part of the catechumen. Its true use seeks to bring each one to real sorrow for sin, a heartfelt trust in the Lord Jesus Christ, and a sincere consecration to Him in loving obedience and service, so that a truly Christian life shall follow, which shall be continually a better and fuller development of the grace of adoption and purification which God has covenanted in holy baptism. Constant care is taken, that in the hands of a spiritual and faithful ministry, this venerable custom of instructing the young and applying the great truths of the gospel to their hearts, may yield its best results, in a well-taught, intelligent and truly spiritual church-membership.

BENEVOLENT WORK.

The General Synod has never forgotten the practical aims to which it was especially consecrated by its organization—the strengthening and enlargement of the Church and the advancement of the Redeemer's kingdom. From the first, and always, it has bent its earnest endeavors to the various forms of Church work that have seemed best adapted to these ends. However imperfectly it has wrought, always falling short of its desires, it has still achieved an unspeakably great service for our Lutheran Church in America, especially in its Anglicized development. Its organization became the source and epoch of a new and energetic Church-life, aggressive activity, and rapid progress over its whole territory.

This benevolent work has been, and is, directed mainly to Education, Home and Foreign Missions, Church Extension, care of Orphans, and Publication and circulation of Church Literature. Following the establishment, already mentioned, of the Theological Seminary at Gettysburg in 1826, directly by the General Synod itself, there were successively founded, under its auspices or by synods or associations connected with the General Synod, Pennsylvania College, Gettysburg, Pa., in 1832; Wittenberg College and Seminary, Springfield, O., in 1845; Roanoke College, Salem, Va., in 1853; Newberry College, at Newberry, S. C., in 1858; North Carolina College, Mount Pleasant, N. C., in 1858; Missionary Institute, Selin's Grove, Pa., in 1858; Carthage College, Carthage, Ill., in 1870; and Watts Memorial College, Guntur, India, in 1886; Midland College, Atchison, Kans., in 1887. Hartwick Seminary was organized in 1815, before the formation of the General Synod, but came, and has remained, under its general auspices. The two Female Seminaries, that at Hagerstown, Md., in 1852, and that at Lutherville, Md., in 1853, are also products of the General Synod church-life and work.

In 1835 the Parent Education Society was formed, which has worked with great efficiency in aiding young men in their preparation for the ministry, though at present the various district synods have committees of their own through which they are conducting this service. In 1835 a Foreign Missionary Society, and in 1845 a Home Missionary Society, were organized under the auspices of the General Synod. Foreign Mission work was established in India in 1842, and in Africa in 1860, which, in both places, has received manifest evidences of divine favor, and developed into large prosperity. A Church Extension Society was organized in 1853, to aid struggling mission congregations in the erection of church edifices. An Orphans' Home was established in 1867, at Loysville, Pa., to whose support and enlargement our eastern Synods regularly contribute. In 1855 the Lutheran Publication Society was organized, the purpose of which is "the diffusion of religious knowledge and the furnishing and circulating of suitable church literature, in harmony with the doctrinal basis of the General Synod of the Evangelical Lutheran Church in the United States." From small beginnings this Society has grown into grand efficiency, circulating an immense amount of our Church literature, and conducting a business through its Publication House that amounted for the year ending March 31, 1891, to $73,200.76, and contributing largely of its profits to the benevolent objects of the Church. In 1843 a Lutheran Historical Society was organized, not indeed as an exclusively General Synod Association, yet originated among its members, with its regular meetings, according to Constitution, held in connection with the conventions of the General Synod. With the active co-operation of members of other Lutheran bodies, there has thus been gathered a Library of Lutheran publications in this country and other materials of American Lutheran history, of priceless value, preserved in the Theological Seminary at Gettysburg. The Woman's Home and Foreign Missionary Society, formed in 1877, to co-operate with the General Synod's Boards, deserves, by its strength and efficiency, to be named among the important organizations of the Church.

The simple enumeration of these educational institutions and other agencies of religious work thus established, can only faintly suggest the splendid development of the Christian life, activity, resources and power which the General Synod has, through them, accomplished for our Church in this land. These institutions, all of them doing efficient service, and some of them growing into proportions of great power and prominence, are sending their blessed influence from shore to shore, and across the seas, and honoring our Church in the face of the whole nation. All these agencies taken together have given us most that is encouraging and cheering in the present possibilities and prospects of our Church, placing it on the high road to the proper accomplishment of its divinely-given mission and work in our land.

CHURCH BOARDS.

The General Synod, since 1871, conducts its work of Foreign Missions, Home Missions, and Church Extension through BOARDS appointed and controlled by itself,—superseding with these the Societies of earlier date. Under the zealous management of these Boards, constituted of prudent and earnest ministers and laymen in equal number, these great departments of Church benevolence and enterprise have been rapidly developed and brought to a most encouraging efficiency. By this method of carrying on these leading forms of benevolent work, the Church's efforts in each of them can be best harmonized and unified, and all the details consistently directed to the surest and largest results. The actual results are strongly testifying to the wisdom of the method. The following statistics of contributions, at intervals of ten years, will give some idea of the immense progress the body is making in its benevolent work—the figures in every case expressing the contributions for two years:

Foreign Missions.

1871 . . . . $13,540.
1881 . . . . 32,133.
1891 . . . . 97,543.

Home Missions.

1871	$21,767.
1881	26,190.
1891	75,974.

Church Extension.

1871	$5,928.
1881	23,405.
1891	79,855.

THE ENGLISH LANGUAGE.

The General Synod has not only been the pioneer in the Anglicizing process among our churches, but it in fact embraces the great body of the English-speaking Lutherans in the United States. It peculiarly represents this idea and its results, and looks upon this as one portion of its great and special mission for the proper prosperity, rank and power of our Lutheran Church in this land. For our true position and influence cannot be rightly achieved as a Church of an alien tongue or of alien tongues. However interesting and adapted to present necessities our Church's polyglot character may now be, the attainment of its right rank and influence in this country requires it to become as rapidly as possible an English-speaking Church. The General Synod keeps this steadily and practically in view. Though neither insensible nor indifferent to the spiritual interests and welfare of the thousands and thousands of Lutherans of other tongues that annually come to these shores, and though rejoicing in their numbers and prosperity, and glad to have their churches or synods in connection with itself, yet, in the position in which Providence has placed it, the General Synod feels that, linguistically, it must stand mainly for the unification and life of our Church as a Church of this English-speaking nation.

AMERICAN.

The General Synod holds that the Lutheran Church, which consists not at all in any accidents of language or other peculiarities of the nation or land of its denominational birth, but in the maintenance of the full, pure gospel of salvation it confesses and preaches, has a world-wide adaptation and vocation. Not, therefore, in the sense of a rupture from its system of doctrine and true principles of its application, but as adapting itself to the new and peculiar conditions and life of our own country, it assumes that the Lutheran Church here must be an American Church. It cannot take its proper place or accomplish its true work in and for our land, if it insists on being a *foreign Church*, whether in language or in any of the other incidental features that may have become associated with its order, customs or life in German or Scandinavian nationalities. In things not of the essence of Lutheranism, the Church must stand in touch with American life. A foreign spirit or type is isolation and displacement from our Church's right relation for its true spiritual vocation here—a maladjustment for effective work and full service. In this sense the General Synod stands for an *American* Lutheran Church.

RELATION TO NON-LUTHERAN DENOMINATIONS.

Mindful of our Saviour's prayer for the unity of His followers (John xvii. 21, 23), the General Synod, in its Constitution (Art. IV., Sec. 7), prescribes for itself the duty of being "*sedulously and incessantly regardful of the circumstances of the times, and of every casual rise and progress of unity of sentiment among Christians in general, in order that the blessed opportunities to promote concord and unity, and the interests of the Redeemer's kingdom, may not pass by neglected and unavailing.*" In accordance with this, and not holding that the Lutheran Church is the only Christian Church, the General Synod cultivates fraternal relations with the other branches of orthodox Protestantism. While holding the truth as our Church confesses it, and thus witnessing against contrary views, it still "believes in one holy Catholic Church," "which is gathered from every nation under the sun," "the congregation of saints, confessing one gospel, having the same knowledge of Christ, and one Holy Spirit, who renews, sanctifies and rules their hearts" (Apol. Conf., Arts. VII. and VIII.). The General Synod, therefore, confessing thus the essential oneness of believers in the one divine Head of the Church, practically also recognizes this spiritual and real brotherhood. It maintains fraternal correspondence, or interchange of courtesies by delegates, with the General Assembly of the Presbyterian Church, the General Assembly of the United Presbyterian Church, the Reformed (Dutch) Church in America, the Reformed (German) Church in the United States, and the General Conference of the United Brethren Church. It enacts no restrictive law against fellowship in pulpit or at altar, but allows to both ministers and members the freedom of conscience and love in this matter.

THE OUTLOOK.

The General Synod, thus organized upon a basis which secures at once the Lutheran system of doctrine and the true catholicity of our Church, and presenting the cheering spectacle of a union of twenty-five prosperous and growing synods which represent the great body of the English-speaking Lutherans in the United States, actuated by intelligent zeal in developing the Church's resources and activities for its best enlargement and prosperity and the extension of the Redeemer's kingdom, with efficient Colleges and Seminaries and Boards and other agencies of success and strength, all wisely adjusted to the conditions for effective service and permanent growth, influence, and power in America, is justly regarded as having been providentially prepared and divinely intended for leadership in achieving the mission and work of the Lutheran Church in this country. The General Synod believes that the great future of our Church in the United States belongs to and is reached by the line of movement marked out in the principles, ideas, and spirit of this general organization. Its catholic Lutheran basis, offering the only hope of union, and its practical principles, adjusting it to our land and times, are prophetic of its great and blessed providential task, and warrant the belief that it represents, in its general and essential characteristics, the great Lutheran Church of the coming centuries in America. In this conception, it holds the maintenance of its permanent existence and integrity as a sacred privilege and duty.

THE GERMAN IOWA SYNOD.

BY

REV. PROF. S. FRITSCHEL, D. D.

THE Synod of Iowa and Adjacent States, which at the present time numbers nearly 300 ministers, embraces six districts covering an area comprising twelve States and Territories, from Ohio to Washington, and from Minnesota and Dakota down to Missouri and Kentucky, and was founded the 24th of August, 1854, by three ministers, one candidate (who was to go as missionary to the Indians), and one lay delegate. All the members of the newly organized body were sent from Germany by the Rev. W. Loehe and the Society for Home Missions of the Lutheran Church in Bavaria. This Society previously, in connection with the Missouri Synod, had been doing a blessed missionary work among the immigrants in the central States of the Union. It represented a strictly confessional as well as œcumenical Lutheranism. The work thus commenced was to be carried on by the Iowa Synod. The congregation at St. Sebald, Ia., a Lutheran

Church colony in whose midst the organization of the Synod took place, and the Theological Seminary at Dubuque, Ia., which was to furnish ministers for the missionary work of the Synod, were founded by Loehe. Indeed, the organization of the Synod itself took place under his advice and auspices, as had been the case before when the Missouri Synod was established. This connection with Loehe has given to the Synod from its very beginning the peculiar churchly character, which in the course of time, though developed and set forth more distinctly, it has always faithfully preserved.

I. Its first synodical declaration was an *unreserved acknowledgment of the Confessions of the Lutheran Church.* This is the unalterable basis of the Constitution of the Synod, as well as of its congregations. The Synod as such accepts the *whole of the Symbolical Books,* as contained in the Concordia of 1580, whilst as to the Constitutions of the individual congregations, an explicit acknowledgment of the unaltered Augsburg Confession and of Luther's Catechism is considered sufficient, because by such acknowledgment the congregations, on their part, implicitly accept the whole of the Lutheran Confessions. The Synod does not want to have this Confession accepted only as to single portions or its essential parts, *but fully and in all its doctrines.* It acknowledges just as explicitly its *thetical* as its *antithetical* decisions and declarations. It confesses what the Lutheran Symbols *confess*, over against the corresponding error, and *rejects with equal decidedness* all errors *rejected* by them. It discountenances every acceptance of the Lutheran Symbols by which they are accepted with the reservation *as far as* they are in harmony with the "Word of God," because by this their conformity with the Scriptures would be put in question; on the contrary, it accepts them as its own Confession, *because* it is convinced of their conformity with the Scripture. This Confession, therefore, is as well its *rule* of all teaching and practice in the church as also the *bond of church fellowship*. The Synod does not allow in its midst any doctrine or administration of the Sacraments, any church- or text-books, any regulations pertaining to divine service, that would be antagonistic to the Symbols, and it makes it the duty of its Presidents and Visitors to see that no deviations of this kind be permitted. And whilst on the one hand it readily *holds fellowship*, especially altar fellowship, with such as are one with it in faith and confession, though they may differ in unessential points, yet on the other hand it must, for the sake of truth, and on account of the great importance of the Confession, *deny* fellowship to those that do not accept the same Confession with it. According to the Constitutions of Synod and congregations, only such persons can be admitted *as members* of a congregation, who accept the Confession of the Lutheran church; and only such *congregations* as make the Lutheran Confession their own can be admitted as members of synod. And only such *ministers* as bind themselves to the Concordia are intrusted with the ministry.

However, in assigning this dominating position to the Confessions, the Iowa Synod has always tried to guard against the *exaggerations* by which the Confessions are put *on a level* with the Word of God, and are given a weight which is due only to the latter. The synod is in earnest when it confesses that the *Holy Scriptures* are the only true rule by which all teachers and all doctrines are to be measured and judged, and it does not derive the normative authority of the teachings of the Confession from the fact that they are the decisions of the Church, but from the fact that they are the *pure and genuine exposition and interpretation of the Divine Word*. It has therefore in all its practice followed a biblical-practical course, and has tried, guided by the Confessions, to recur in all cases and questions, to the Scriptures themselves, and to draw from them directly. The Symbols are not considered, like the Scriptures, as judges, but as a witness and declaration of the faith, as to how at any time the Holy Scriptures have been understood and explained in the articles in controversy in the church of God by those who then lived, and how the opposite dogma was rejected and condemned. On account of this historical view of the Symbols, the Iowa Synod does not see in them a code of law of atomistic dogmas of equal value and equal weight, but an organic expression of the living connection of the faith of the Church. Accordingly, there is a distinction to be made between the *dogmas, properly speaking, and other parts of the Symbols;* as e. g. the frequent exegetical, historical and other deductions, illustrations and demonstrations. Only the former, i. e. the dogmas, constitute the Confession, whilst the latter partake of this dignity only indirectly, inasmuch as they define the dogmas more clearly. What the Symbols state and intend *as a confession*, the articles and doctrines of faith, this it is, to which the Synod is bound, not because they are the Church's decisions of the controversies that have come up, but because they present the saving truth and doctrine of the Scripture. The Church is bound to accept these doctrines which constitute the Confession in their totality, *without exception*, whilst the demand of doctrinal conformity by no means includes *all unessential* opinions which *are only occasionally* mentioned in the Symbols. Thus e. g. the obligation to the Symbols by no means refers equally to the article concerning the conception of Christ by the Holy Ghost, and to the doctrine of the perpetual virginity of Mary, though the latter occasionally occurs in the Smalcald Articles. This would be a legalistic misuse of the Symbols against which the Iowa Synod has always protested.

The Synod however is far from being satisfied with a merely formal adherence to the Confessions. It does not wish to lay up the inheritance of pure doctrine and faith which we have received from our fathers in a napkin, but considers it as a pound which is to be employed most profitably. It discountenances all dead orthodoxy, and next to the purity of doctrine and a scriptural administration of the sacraments it lays all stress upon showing the faith *in a Christian life.* It emphasizes true conversion, repentance and faith, by personal assurance of salvation and a godly life. It has from its beginning tried to enforce *strict church discipline* in its congregations, and their Constitutions require of those who seek to be admitted to membership evidence of a Christian life. Such discipline it also endeavors to enforce in regard to *secret societies,* against which its congregations are earnestly warned. In all relations of Christian and church-life it urges the necessity of showing the true faith in good works: in rendering aid to its needy members, widows and orphans, in the work of Home and Foreign Missions, and in fostering a proper arrangement of Christian worship, and a right development of the congregational and churchly life in general. From the beginning the Synod has designated this tendency as a striving after a more perfect development of the Lutheran Church. Although we must lament that in all these points the ideal aimed at has not as yet been attained, nevertheless the Synod is still striving for this object with untiring zeal. She also is striving after a growing richer and deeper knowledge, but only on the basis of the Symbols under the guidance of the divine Word.

If, therefore, on the one hand, the synod decidedly rejects every imaginary progress and every so-called development of the dogma, antagonistic to the Confession, it acknowledges on the other hand as true progress and development in the right direction, all development that grows out of this principle and stays within the limits of the same. To such progress the synod is open, for such there is room in it, and within these limits it is striving for a greater perfection.

2. Out of this fundamental confessional position of the Iowa Synod there neccessarily results the attitude it has assumed in the several controversies in which it has been involved. The organization of the Iowa Synod was caused by the fact that the Missouri Synod in its controversy with the Synod of Buffalo concerning the *Church and the ministry*, would no longer suffer in its midst nor admit to its membership the men sent by Loehe who would not agree with Missouri's views. Then, as they could neither side with Buffalo nor with Missouri they commenced a new, independent activity further West. Thus the synod found itself in its very incipiency involved in a doctrinal controversy in which the principal point between itself and Mis-

souri was the so-called *Uebertragungslehre*, the doctrine concerning the conferring of the office upon the minister. The Iowa Synod rejected the view according to which the ministerial office is derived from the invisible church, that it is originally vested in the individual members of the same in their spiritual priesthood, and by them conferred upon the ministers of the Church through their vocation to the Holy office. The Iowa Synod agreed with Missouri in so far as it taught that the holy office was originally and directly given by God to the Church, but differed from Missouri in so far as it maintained that the office was given to the Church in its totality, not to its single members, and that the Church possessed the office in and with the means of grace, not in the spiritual priesthood and in the state of grace of its true members. And if the conferring of the office takes place in accordance with a regular call by a single congregation, it is not on account of the true members of the invisible Church that may be hidden in it, but because the Church, which in its totality possesses the office and which is as well invisible communion of the Spirit as visible communion of the means of grace, is in its totality and essence existing even in the smallest individual congregation, where two or three are gathered together in the name of Jesus. The principal interest which the Iowa Synod had in this controversy was, however, to *assert the princi-*

ple that it is sufficient for church-unity to agree in the doctrine of the Confession that the office was given to the Church, not to single persons, and that a difference of opinion as to the farther theological exposition of this doctrine did not destroy the unity of faith and confession, and that it, therefore, must not stand in the way of a mutual recognition as brethren in the faith. This is the *position of the Synod* in the controversy concerning the holy office. It is evident at a glance that this is merely the consequence of its attitude to the Confessions.

3. Quite a similar position the Synod has taken concerning the doctrine of the millennium. This controversy also was forced upon it from outside. When Chiliasm, which had formerely been tolerated by the Missouri Synod, was prescribed by it, and the Rev. Schieferdecker expelled, the latter applied to the Iowa Synod, and asked whether they considered him a heretic, who must be denied church-fellowship on account of his view of the Millennium. As the Synod, according to its confessional standpoint, answered this question negatively, it was accused of holding an un-Lutheran view with regard to the Millennium. This compelled the Synod to defend its position on this question, and to explain *the kind* of eschatological opinions or doctrines for which it claimed the toleration of the Church. It protested against the insinuation that this presentation of the doctrines

of the conversion of Israel, of Antichrist, and his destruction at the second coming of Christ, of the Millennium and the first resurrection, were a *synodical confession*, and that consequently, Chiliasm was made a synodical dogma. Only what the Confessions state of the Last Things it wanted to be considered as its own confession. Accordingly it *rejected* every view of the Millennium by which the spiritual kingdom of God during that period would be made an outward worldly kingdom, and in which the Church would not be essentially and principally a communion of faith; in general— every view according to which there would be another way of salvation in that period than in the present. On the other hand, Synod *declared* that it could not reject the doctrines mentioned above, concerning the conversion of Israel, etc., as heresies which would destroy church-fellowship, as long as they were free from the characteristics of a fanatical view of Chiliasm as given in the Symbols. So long as such fanatical views were not entertained, it declared there was room in the Synod for these opinions as well as for the opposing antichiliastic ones, and in such difference of opinion it could not see a prejudice to the necessary unity of faith. Its reason for taking this position was, that in this case the point in question was not the dogma, but theological problems in regard to which, notwithstanding the fullest harmony in the Confessions, there may be a difference of opinion. On account of such differences, church-fellowship which rests only upon the Confession itself, must not be denied.

4. The doctrines of the conversion of Israel, the Millennium and the first resurrection, are not referred in any of the symbolical statements. But the Antichrist is spoken of at different places, and the Smalcald Articles declare, not only occasionally but directly, that the Pope is the true *Antichrist*. The Iowa Synod has, therefore, been claimed as being in direct opposition to the Confession, because it does not see the Antichrist solely and exclusively in the Pope, but declares the opinion may be tolerated in the Church according to which a personal Antichrist is expected in the Last Times. But also on this question the Iowa Synod fully accepts all the declarations of the Confessions. They do, however, not teach that the Antichrist is solely and exclusively the Pope. The Confessions do not teach that the Antichrist is the Pope, but that the Pope is the Antichrist; and far from seeing the Antichrist exclusively in the Pope, they rather state at another place that Popery is a *part* of the Antichrist's kingdom. The statement that popery is an entire subversion of Christianity, consequently Antichristendom as prophesied in Holy Scripture, is indeed just as much a part of the confession of faith as the rejection of false doctrine. But the questions whether Antichrist be a collective term only or also an individual person—whether

the prophecy concerning the same be wholly fulfilled or whether some future fulfillment is yet to be expected—are exegetical problems which have not been considered by the Confessions. The Iowa Synod therefore does not in the least disagree with the Confession, when on the one hand it accepts all the assertions of the Confessions covering the antichristian character of Popery, and on the other hand regards the questions mentioned above as open ones, without a confessional character, and therefore without affecting the unity of the Church, tolerates the opinion that Anti-christ is yet to be expected, along with that that the Roman Pontiff is exclusively Antichrist.

5. The position which the Iowa Synod has taken in these controverted questions is only the natural consequence of the principle, which even without regard to its special application it professes in general: *i. e.* the recognizing of *open questions*. The more earnestly it emphazises, over against unionism, the necessity for church-unity of agreement in the doctrine, and declares it to be absolutely necessary to church-fellowship, the more earnest are also its endeavors to avoid sectarian exaggeration. The Augsburg Confession declares; "To the true unity of the Church it is enough to agree concerning the doctrine of the Gospel and the administration of the sacraments," that is, to agree in the doctrine of salvation and of faith. Herein is implied the further declaration

that an agreement must not necessarily exist in such doctrines which are not doctrines of faith. The Iowa Synod accordingly *declares* that for church-fellowship there must be required *no absolute* agreement in doctrine, but only an agreement in the doctrine of faith; but this indeed in the *whole* doctrine of faith, and in *all* its articles. This doctrine of faith forms the contents of the Confessions, and consequently the sum total of the doctrines of the Confessions is the indispensable extent of agreement in doctrine. There must however not be inferred from this, that these doctrines are indispensable and binding doctrines of faith because they are found in the Symbols of the Church, and that the decision of the Church which is expressed by the Symbols gives them the value and validity of divinely certain and binding doctrines of salvation. On the contrary, the Church has laid them down in its Confessions only because they are the doctrines of Scripture, on which saving faith depends. On the other hand, the Iowa Synod *rejects* the opinion that an agreement also in such doctrines of Scripture which are no doctrines of faith be *conditio sine qua non* of church-fellowship, and that church-fellowship must be dissolved on their account. If there be agreement, in all other respects, in the doctrine of the Confessions, and there only remains a difference in other points, the Synod will tolerate this and regard them as open questions. This does not mean that we should not strive for agreement even in such doctrines as e. g. *Uebertragungslehre*, conversion of Israel, Antichrist, etc., or that theological controversies concerning them are useless and harmful. Neither are they, by styling them open questions, declared to be doubtful and uncertain doctrines, concerning which a definite and certain persuasion cannot be attained, and by no means does this import that they could arbitrarily be adopted or rejected. But this only is the meaning of that expression, that these doctrines, on which there is in fact a diversity of opinion even among those who fully agree in the Confessions, must not be regarded as *church-dividing*, and that a difference of their conception can be allowed, because they are no doctrines of faith, and there can be from their very nature no certainty of faith concerning them, as they are also not taught in Scripture as clearly and distinctly as the doctrine of faith. The Iowa Synod has mainly been induced to hold this position by the earnest desire to prevent the doctrinal and confessional basis of the Lutheran Church from being rendered doubtful in its divine certainty by having mixed with it merely theological views and opinions, and from having destroyed thereby its fundamental character, according to which it forms or dissolves church-fellowship.

6. Whilst the Iowa Synod will not suffer anything to be added to this basis, it objects also to having anything taken away, and will not allow

any doctrine of the Confessions to be made an open question. On account of this position the Synod was moved to take the stand which it has held in the *Predestinarian controversy*. Soon after the Missourian Predestinatianism had appeared for the first time in 1868, the Iowa Synod opposed it and repudiated it as a deviation from the doctrine of the Confessions. The Synod was well aware even in the doctrine of Predestination that there were points which must be considered open questions, as e. g. the distinction made between election in its wider or stricter sense, as well as between *voluntas antecedens* and *consequens*, the teaching that election has taken place *intuitu fidei*, implying that faith is the condition or the instrumental or the subordinate impulsive cause of election, etc. But from the very beginning Predestinarianism was pronounced by the Synod to be apostasy from the Confessions and a church-dividing error. The Iowa Synod by no means holds that predestination signifies only the general decree to save all men through faith in Christ, which God eternally has decreed, but it teaches that it really is an *individual* Predestination, and if a man is saved, it avows this to be the *effect* of this decree on him, and the cause thereof to be no other than this eternal, effective, gracious will of God, and in no way man's own will, self-determination and merit. But it condemns the doctrine that Predestination of individuals or election is a decree essentially *different from the universal decree* of grace which God has decreed *outside* of and *aside* of and *in addition* to the universal one, so that there be found in God a contradicting will, a universal one and one not universal. Over against this it maintains that individual predestination has taken place *within* the universal decree of God, is contained in it, and *no other will* than this same universal decree itself, however with a *special reference*, namely, inasmuch as it refers to the children of God in special, as they are known by God before the foundation of the world. It prefers that mode of teaching, which represents predestination as the applying of the universal decree to the individual, in whom the same becomes realized, which works his salvation and everything thereto pertaining, consequently also the saving faith, and prefers it because by this mode also the comforting power of predestination is rendered prominent. It allows however also the other mode of teaching, which takes predestination in its narrower sense, strictly as the election of a definite number of certain men from the great mass of reprobates, if there be also taught that Predestination in this sense has taken place *intuitu fidei*. The Synod however rejects the opinion that discriminating selection of some before others has been made *without regard* to man's conduct, merely according to the pleasure of the will of God, and holds that this can be asserted of Predestination only when it is taken in accordance with the mode of teaching mentioned in the first place, as the universal decree referring and applied to individuals. And whilst it asserts Predestination in the latter meaning to be the *source* of our salvation as well as of *our faith* and our persevering in the same, it denies that predestination being taken merely as selection is the *cause* of some believing and others abiding in unbelief. It rejects the opinion that even the most obdurate resistance of those who were ordained by this selection will not hinder it from making them believers and save them, and maintains that on the contrary the obdurate resistance of the reprobates, which God has foreknown, has prevented Him from predestinating them in His eternal decree. It disowns the opinion that the effect of universal grace is indeed exhibited and manifested in the faith of those who believe for a time, but that perseverance in faith is the effect of selecting grace alone. And concerning the appealing to the secret will of God, the Iowa Synod unreservedly recognizes the manifold unsearchable problems which pertain to it, but denies that the cause of God's not having elected all men, and of His not taking away the resistance even from the reprobates is His secret will, according to which He will not do with them what He does with His elect, as it is distinctly revealed that the cause thereof is not in God, but in the persevering self-hardening of man. On the other hand it is indeed concealed in the secret foreknowledge of

God who of those *who* are called will believe, and *who* not, and *who* of the converted will persevere, and *who* will not. And as God has reserved these secrets for His wisdom, and has not revealed them, according to the doctrine of the Iowa Synod the elect can indeed be *absolutely* sure of their election and preservation on the part of God, but not on their part of their persevering in faith, because the revelation of the decree of predestination on which rests the certainty of perseverance of the elect runs thus, that God would support His work in them to the end, *if* they observe God's Word, pray diligently, abide in God's goodness, and faithfully use the gifts received. This is the position the Iowa Synod holds in regard to Predestinationism at large, and in its particulars, and in this manner it has endeavored to enforce the Confessions as the indispensable foundations of doctrine also in this special point over against Predestinarianism, which is fundamentally opposed to the same.

7. In a different manner it has pursued this aim, by taking the position which it holds in regard to the *General Council.* In consequence of its confessional principles it hailed with joy the attempt to unite the Lutheran Church of our country on the basis of the Confessions, the *whole* of the Confessions, and the Confessions *alone.* Though it would have preferred a Free Conference as a preliminary step, yet it was not averse to the idea

of founding a General Council, when from another quarter it was claimed that this was complying with a deep-felt want and that the necessary conditions therefor existed. According to its principles of Confession, however, it could join such a General Body only if the same would recognize also the Lutheran Confessions as the Church-uniting and Church-dividing basis, and repudiate mixed communion and exchange of pulpits with those of another faith. The General Council, however, was not prepared to do this, and the Iowa Synod accordingly was compelled to defer its full connection with the same. It did, however, not withdraw entirely, but entered into a relation to it which has been provided for by the constitution of the General Council, and by which the Synod was enabled to take part not only with its foreign missionary, liturgical work, etc., but also with the debates on the topics of mixed communion and exchange of pulpits which since that time for a number of years took place at the conventions of the General Council. All the time its exertions were directed to demonstrating the principle of the indispensable restriction of church-fellowship to those who are of the same faith as is implied in the acceptance of the same Confessions and in the holding of the same confessional basis. The Synod was and is persuaded, that it adds no new condition of Church-fellowship at all to the Confessions but that it merely asserts the inevitable consequence of the same, which is directly contained therein. For the participating in the confessional act of celebrating the Lord's Supper is a *real and very emphatic confession*, and the *principle* that only those who are of the same household of faith may partake of it, whilst those of another faith must be excluded, is nothing else but the " we believe and profess," "we reject and condemn," of the Confessions themselves in their *direct application to ecclesiastical practice*. The Iowa Synod was well aware that the bad custom of mixed communion and exchange of pulpits which has crept in would not at once everywhere be discontinued, and that such deviations from the principle occurring now and then within the limits of the different Synods should be no reason against entering into a closer union with them. But the acknowledgment of the principle that church-fellowship—fellowship in the Lord's Supper and the pulpit—could be claimed and granted only on the basis of unity in Confession, it declared to be indispensable, since it pertained to the necessary confessional basis. On this account the different and successive declarations of the General Council, though the Iowa Synod would not hesitate to acknowledge the progress made, did not suffice, as they rather dwelt on the pastoral duty in regard to the application of this principle and the dealing with exceptions, instead of unreservedly confessing this principle itself. Not before the clear and plain Confession of the Swedish Augustana Synod concerning this question had been endorsed by the General Council at Galesburg, 1875, and the rule: "Lutheran pulpits for Lutheran ministers only and Lutheran altars for Lutheran communicants only," had been declared to be founded upon *the Word of God and the Confessions* of our Church, did the Iowa Synod hold that the confessional principle was recognized, which at Fort Wayne, 1867, it had urged as the indispensable condition on which the official union of Synods might be effected. This Galesburg rule was strongly opposed in different parts of the General Council. The proceedings, however, which took place at the successive meetings of the General Council, and which were based upon the theses of the sainted Dr. Krauth, who treated the question of altar and pulpit fellowship with incomparable clearness, served to foster the expectation that this opposition would be overcome more and more, and the Galesburg rule gain universal and approved acceptance. The Iowa Synod already declared that it was hindered no longer from organically uniting with the General Council by confessional scruples, as at Galesburg the Confessional principle, which it considered to be indispensable, had been adopted. Since that time, however, within the General Council things seem to have undergone a change. The understanding of the Galesburg rule, as the official acknowledgment of the principle set forth by the Iowa Synod at Fort Wayne, has repeatedly and very emphatically been opposed by very influential parties, and declined by them in the name of the General Council. These declarations have, indeed, been contradicted just as emphatically by other parties. But since they have not yet been renounced by the General Council itself, the Iowa Synod is induced to be more cautious in asserting that the necessary conditions for full Church union exist. It is now waiting for future development within the General Council, still hoping for a final official declaration in favor of the Confessional principle of unmixed communion and pulpit-fellowship. Whatever this final decision may be—this principle is the indispensable condition of all Church union for the Iowa Synod, in accordance with its position to the Confessions.

8. Similarly as regarding doctrine and church-fellowship, the Confessions are also the decisive norm of all *ecclesiastical orders and rites*. In this the Synod has maintained the connection with the older Lutheran Church, and preserved ecclesiastical tradition, as well as taken in account the circumstances of our country.

First of all, the Synod is taking pains to ground and confirm the necessary agreement in faith and confession by a *thorough instruction* in the doctrine of the Church, to which end it emphasizes a careful catechetical instruction aside from the sermon. It urges not only scrupulous instruction by pastors of the catechumens, but also the fostering and upbuilding of those who have been confirmed. It does not neglect Sunday-schools; it desires simply to have them conducted in a strictly Lutheran way. It prefers, however, the reliable and well-approved Church examinations (Christenlehre), and will not have them ranked below the Sunday-school. It also lays great stress on the establishment of parochial schools, and insists on her members sending their children to the same up to the time of their confirmation, as a conscientious duty. Where congregations are yet too small to support parochial teachers, the ministers give instruction in these schools, where special attention is paid to religious instruction. It does not take this course in opposition to the public schools. These are rather considered a great blessing for our civil life and an indispensable institution of our country, which must vigorously be supported against Romish assaults. But since the baptism of infants comprises the obligation of an education in the faith, and the Sunday-school instruction is not sufficient for this purpose, Lutheran parents can make use of schools where religion cannot be taught for their baptized children only when the instruction required by baptism has been brought to a close in confirmation.

Also, in respect to the *order of service* and ministerial acts, the Synod strives to sustain the connection with the Old Church and her liturgical usages, considering, however, at the same time, the circumstances and wants of the time present. From the very beginning Lœhe's Agenda has been used in her congregations, whose liturgy is essentially the same as that of the Church book of the General Council, with whose liturgical principles it is in perfect harmony. This liturgical form is regarded the ideal to which the congregations ought to be brought up, but the Synod claims no governmental powers towards introducing it, and will sooner bear diversity in this respect than injure the liturgical liberty of the individual congregations, contrary to the Confessions of the Church. On this account it also does not insist upon the establishment of Private Confession under all circumstances but where it cannot be established, it only persists the more strenuously on personally giving notice of one's intention to partake of the Lord's Supper, that the examination may take place of which the Confession speaks.

Its *synodical and congregational organization*, lastly, is based upon the Symbolical fundamental principle that all ecclesiastical power be given to the Church principally and immediately, as the same is ecclesiastically represented even in the smallest local church. It therefore acknowledges no other governmental powers of the Synod, but that which has been conferred upon the same by the individual congregations, and it assumes not more than advisory power in regard to congregational affairs. The oversight of its congregations and pastors, with which it is intrusted, is put in practice among other things by visitations, which regularly take place biennially. It strenuously enforces what is *juris divini* in the church order. It rejects the license system, the calling for a certain time, etc., and acknowledges but a regular call by election on the part of the congregation (the president of the synod either proposing for election or ratifying the same) and by ordination and installation on the part of Synod. The annual conventions of its District Synods are composed of the pastors as the representatives of the Ministerium and of one lay delegate for every Synodical congregation as representatives of the same. To the conventions of the General Synod, which occur every three or four years, five ministers and five congregations send one representative respectively. A standing committee or "Synodal Ausschuss" represents the entire Synod during the time intervening between its conventions.

THE GENERAL COUNCIL.

BY

REV. PROF. H. E. JACOBS, D. D., LL. D.

THE General Council makes no claim of comprising within itself all truly Lutheran Synods and churches in America. Nor, if we understand it, does it have any such aim. There is no such thing as a "General Council Lutheran Church." There may be those who have regarded it as destined to supplant or merge within itself all other general bodies, but we are sure that this is not its spirit. Its great purpose is the development of the Lutheran Church of this country, in accordance with the principles of Confessional and Historical Lutheranism. It affords the means whereby any number of Synods that have been brought to a real understanding and a hearty appreciation of each other's position, as true and consistent adherents of the faith confessed at Augsburg, may coöperate harmoniously, until the time come for a wider and more general union. It is pledged to the maintenance of distinctive Lutheranism. Whether this require the permanence of any one particular organization, call it General Council, or General Synod, or Synodical Conference, or anything else, is a matter of relative indifference. It makes no war, therefore, upon any other general body, anxious though it is that all who confess the same faith should recognize and coöperate with one another. It seeks to interfere with the work of no Synods or congregations or individuals claiming to be Lutheran, but not choosing to unite with it. It simply demands that its own work shall be accorded similar respect; and that all who claim recognition as Lutherans do no injury to the common cause by betraying well-established Lutheran principles. It has embodied its entire conception of the nature, modes, conditions and obligations of Church organization in most clear and explicit terms in its "Fundamental Principles of Faith and Church Polity." A statement of these "Fundamental Principles," with a brief exposition of their meaning, will afford the best means of understanding the General Council's position. "The Principles of Faith" are:

"I. There must be and abide through all time, one Holy Christian Church, which is the assembly of all believers, among whom the Gospel is purely preached, and the Holy Sacraments administered, as the Gospel demands.

"To the true unity of the Church, it is sufficient that there be agreement touching the doctrine of the Gospel, that it be preached in one accord in its pure sense, and that the sacraments be administered conformably to God's Word."

This is Article VII of the Augsburg Confession, as it reads in the German text. It affords the definition of the Church, as properly speaking, not an external, visible body, but the sum total of all believers, whoever and wherever they be, "the Communion of Saints," as the Apostles' Creed confesses, or as Luther, in the Smalcald Articles declares: "Thank God, to-day a child seven years old knows what the Church is, viz: saints, believers and lambs, who hear the voice of their Shepherd;" or Melanchthon in the Apology: "This Church exists, viz: the truly believing and righteous men scattered throughout the whole world."

It gives the marks of the Church as "the pure preaching of the Word, and the right administration of the sacraments." For wherever there is true faith there must be also a confession of this faith; and conversely, wherever God gives his Word, the Holy Spirit is ever active and begets a true people of God. God's Word can never be without God's people, or God's people without God's Word. While the Church properly speaking is not visible, and no one can draw the line dividing precisely the believing from the unbelieving, nevertheless, wherever these marks appear, we are sure that the Church is present, even though many externally connected with it be hypocrites. The purity of the preaching also has its degrees. As the Word of God is always efficacious, even when accompanied by error, it is impossible to determine the extent to which such purity may be only relative where a Church really exists. The purer the preaching of the Word and the administration of the sacraments, the purer the Church, the firmer its foundations, the more faithful its testimony, and the more efficacious its work.

If the Church, therefore, be properly the true people of God, the unity of the Church consists in the bond of common faith in Christ, which, by uniting them with Him, unites them also with one another. This unity is promoted by all that strengthens faith in Christ and His word. It is retarded by all that weakens such faith, or recedes from the Gospel. The external expression of this unity consists neither in external organization, whether under a hierarchy, as the Papacy, or in a confederacy of denominations—or Synods; nor in the use of identical ceremonies or forms of worship, however serviceable this may be in promoting good order and a common understanding. "Agreement touching the doctrine of the Gospel," which includes the right administration of the sacraments, is the prime requisite of Church unity and Church union. For in the doctrine of the Gospel we hear Christ's voice, and as every one follows that voice, one impulse from one Spirit influences the entire body, and even without knowing or hearing of one another, "they speak the same thing," and are "perfectly joined together in the same mind and in the same judgment." (1 Cor. i. 10).

"II. The true unity of a particular Church, in virtue of which men are truly members of one and the same Church, and by which any Church abides in real identity, and is entitled to a continuation of her name, is unity in doctrine and faith and in the sacraments."

A distinction between a universal and a particular Church is here affirmed. Different degrees of purity in the preaching of the Gospel and the administration of the sacraments, different degrees of accuracy in defining the doctrines of God's Word and expressing the contents of the one common faith, the exaltation of adiaphora into matters of essential importance, the depreciation of matters of essential importance into adiaphora, the determination of forms of Church government as indispensable conditions of Church unity, even the limitations determined by national or linguistic lines, explain the division of the Church universal into particular churches. But whatever be the principle according to which the separate existence of any particular Church has been established, what is true of the Church Universal is true also of all its parts. Its unity is a "unity in doctrine and faith and in the sacraments." This is further explained:

"That she continues to teach and to set forth, and that her true members embrace from the heart, and use, the articles of faith and the sacraments, as they were held and administered when the Church came into distinctive being and received a distinctive name."

When she teaches otherwise than they taught

who were her historical ancestors, she has broken her unity with them, and is no longer the same Church, no difference though the name be retained, or however preponderant on her side may be numerical majorities. If every member would agree to a change in her Creed, this would not change the testimony of the communion which was fixed at its organization. It would only show that the historical successor was a different Church. The Roman Catholic Church cannot amend the decrees of the Council of Trent, so as to remove elements on which the Tridentine fathers insisted, or to include Protestant conceptions of doctrine, without thereby ceasing to be the same Church as that which for three centuries and a half has recognized those decrees as the standard of teaching, and excluded from the hope of salvation all who disputed their authority. Every particular Church stands for a particular statement or type of doctrine; and the life of that particular Church is maintained or perishes, as the statement or type of doctrine of that particular Church is maintained or surrendered.

"III. The unity of the Church is intrusted to, and made manifest in the solemn, public and official Confessions, which are set forth, to wit: The generic unity of the Christian Church in the general Creeds, and the specific unity of pure parts of the Christian Church in their specific Creeds: one chief object of both classes of which Creeds is, that Christians who are in the unity of faith may know each other as such, and may have a visible bond of fellowship."

"IV. That Confessions may be such a testimony of unity, and bond of union, they must be accepted in every statement of doctrine, in their own true, native, original and only sense. Those who set them forth and use them, must not only agree to use the same words, but must use and understand these words in one and the same sense."

The Confessions, as visible bonds of fellowship, are articles of agreement among those who subscribe them. Like all other contracts, to be of any value, they must be expressed in clear and unambiguous terms. A contract that is capable of being understood in two or more senses by the parties who subscribe it, is utterly worthless, and need not be signed, so far as any value either party to the contract derives from it. An article of agreement, whether in Civil Law or in Church Organization, reaches its end only when both parties understand its terms "in one and the same sense." To ask men to sign a document, with the understanding that the meaning intended to be conveyed by those who framed it need not be accepted, but that every one is free to attach to it his own interpretation, is an attempt to defeat the very end for which the document was framed. It is equivalent to using bushels of varying capacities, or yard-sticks of different lengths. The famous Tract XCI., by the late Cardinal Newman, was an effort to show how men could subscribe the XXXIX Articles of the Church of England, and put upon them a Romanizing interpretation, *i. e.*, remain in the Church of England while being at heart Romanists. The effort is here made to prevent any such procedure in the churches uniting in the General Council. It is not subscription to Confessions of faith that is desired, so much as to the faith of the Confessions. The unity of the Church does not consist in subscription to the same Confessions, but in the acceptance and teaching of the same doctrines. Where the doctrines of the Confessions are not believed, it is the solemn duty of the person who questions them to testify on all occasions against them, instead of seeking to hide his dissent under an ambiguous or indefinite formula. The right of private judgment must be constantly guaranteed; but this right demands that Confessions shall be subscribed only after they have been tested by the study of the Holy Scripture, and their entire Scriptural character has been determined. In other words, "that Confessions be a bond of union," they must be recognized as the expressions of an agreement that is deeper and firmer than that of the mere document that is recognized and subscribed.

"V. The unity of the Evangelical Lutheran Church, as a portion of the Holy Christian Church, depends upon her abiding in one and the same faith, in confessing which she obtained her distinctive name, her political recognition, and her history."

Thus it is explicitly declared, that the Evangelical Lutheran Church does not contain all Christians, but is only a portion of the Holy Christian Church. We know of no one in the

General Council who has ever taught otherwise. Should there, however, at any time be such a one among us, his teaching would directly contradict a principle, which the General Council requires every Synod uniting with it to adopt.

But where the faith of the Lutheran Church is amended or modified, while the bounds of the Holy Christian Church may not be transcended, the unity of Lutheranism is undoubtedly broken. If the faith be not the same faith which gave the Lutheran Church its distinctive position, just in so far there is no unity with the Lutheran Church. However high the position which a teacher may be accorded within what calls itself the Lutheran Church, if he hold and teach *e. g.* that original sin is not truly sin, or that Christ has not made a sacrifice for all the sins of men, or that some merit is connected with human preparations for God's grace, or that the Holy Spirit does not ordinarily work through the Word and sacraments, or that faith is sometimes without good works, or that some other requirements besides agreement concerning the Gospel and sacraments are necessary to the unity of the Church, or that no grace is offered in Baptism, or that there is no real presence in the Holy Supper, etc., he has broken the unity of the Lutheran Church. If all our general bodies, viz., General Synod, General Council, Synodical Conference, United Synod, Ohio, Iowa, Norwegian Conference, etc., were to unite in a unanimous rejection of some distinctive feature of the Lutheran Church of the Reformation period, they could not change the faith and confession of the Lutheran Church, but would simply demonstrate that in such action these bodies were no longer Lutheran, but had broken with the unity of the Lutheran Church. The unity of the Lutheran, as a particular Church, is found only in consistent adherence to her historical position, and in progress on the lines of her historical development.

> "VI. The unaltered Augsburg Confession is by preëminence the Confession of that faith. The acceptance of its doctrines and the avowal of them without equivocation or mental reservation, make, mark and identify that Church which alone in the true, original, historical and honest sense of the term is the Evangelical Lutheran Church."

It is well to notice that it is not the acceptance of the unaltered Augsburg Confession, but the acceptance of its *doctrines*, which determines the Lutheran character of a teacher or Church body. A man who has never subscribed the Augsburg Confession, or even never seen it, is a Lutheran, if he teach the doctrines which it maintains. A man who makes his subscription to the Confession an object of especial boast, is no Lutheran, if "by equivocation or mental reservation," or even by excusable misunderstanding, he depart from any of the doctrines therein clearly and professedly taught. He may hold or not hold to additional confessions; he may see or may deny their importance. The question as to whether he be a Lutheran or not, the General Council affirms, must be decided from his relation to the doctrines of the unaltered Augsburg Confession, and from no other standard whatever. "The *doctrines* of the unaltered Augsburg Confession—nothing more, nothing less." This is all that the General Council demands, as the test of what is Lutheran. Hence its "principles" continue:

"VII. The only Churches, therefore, of any land, which are properly in the unity of that communion, and by consequence entitled to its name, Evangelical Lutheran, are those which sincerely hold and truthfully confess the doctrines of the unaltered Augsburg Confession.

"VIII. We accept and acknowledge the doctrines of the unaltered Augsburg Confession in its original sense, as throughout in conformity with the pure truth of which God's Word is the only rule. We accept its statements of truth as in perfect accordance with the canonical Scriptures. We reject the errors it condemns, and believe that all which it commits to the liberty of the Church, of right belongs to that liberty."

But while thus maintaining that the acceptance of the doctrines of the Augsburg Confession is enough to decide the Lutheran character of a teacher or a Church or a Synod, nevertheless, where the doctrines of the Augsburg Confession have been called into question and involved in controversy, and where the Confession has been subscribed by those who disbelieved and doubted its doctrines, and who attempted to justify their subscription upon the plea that they were at liberty to make their own interpretation of the meaning of the Confession, and that the Confession could be properly subscribed at the same time by parties holding diverse views of what it meant, it has at times become necessary to restate the doctrines of the unaltered Confession in ampler Confessions. These add nothing to the Augsburg Confession, but only guard it from ambiguities. The arguments and illustrations which they give are not the proper objects of the subscription. All that is to be determined is the true meaning of the Augsburg Confession. As the entire principle of Confessional subscription, according to which Confessions, as contracts, are to be understood only in the sense given them by those who first published them, has been so often violated with respect to the Augsburg Confession, it becomes necessary for the Church to know, with respect to each of its ministers, as to what is the construction which he puts upon it. Hence the Apology, the Smalcald Articles, the Catechisms of Luther and the Formula of Concord, are adopted as consistent exhibitions and defences of the doctrines taught in the Fundamental Confession. The last of these "Principles," therefore, is:

"IX. In thus formally accepting and acknowledging the unaltered Augsburg Confession, we declare our conviction that the other Confessions of the Evangelical Lutheran Church, inasmuch as they set forth none other than its system of doctrine, and articles of faith, are of necessity pure and Scriptural."

This sentence must be placed alongside of Principle VII above given. By "other Confessions of the Evangelical Lutheran Church," those are meant "which sincerely hold and truthfully confess the doctrines of the unaltered Augsburg Confession." Any one familiar with the Lutheran "Church Orders," whose confession has been made the standard of the "Common Service" by General Synod, General Council and United Synod, can give an account of the doctrinal formulas which are included in most of them, intended to promote the pure teaching of the doctrines of the Augsburg Confession in the respective Lutheran countries for which the "Orders" were prepared. They are examples of the "other Confessions." All such Confessions, then, as harmonize with the doctrines of the Augsburg Confession, the General Council acknowledges as "of necessity pure and Scriptural." All Confessions, whether of the Lutheran name or not, that do not harmonize therewith, it rejects and condemns.

"Preëminent among such accordant, pure and Scriptural statements of doctrine, by their intrinsic excellence, by the great and necessary ends for which they were prepared, by their historical position, and by the general judgment of the Church, are these: the Apology of the Augsburg Confession, the Smalcald Articles, the Catechisms of Luther and the Formula of Concord, all of which are, with the unaltered Augsburg Confession, in the perfect harmony of one and the same Scriptural faith."

This reference to the full body of Confessions

contained in the "Book of Concord" is intended for the ministry, and not for the laity. It is understood that greater demands must be made of a public teacher than of private members, of professors of theology than of pastors; just as in civil life, only those "learned in the law" are competent for positions as judges, or even as attorneys, and, therefore, must be subjected to a special examination. It is presupposed that every candidate for the Lutheran ministry has spent sufficient time in preparation for his work to learn the history of the doctrines of the Augsburg Confession in their relation to subsequent controversies and to be ready to declare where a statement of the results of those controversies can be found.

Taking the fullest of these Confessions, the Formula of Concord, as an example, we may briefly review its office and significance. 1. It teaches that consistency with the doctrines of the Augsburg Confession requires us, on the one hand, to reject the view that, since the fall, man's nature is sin, and on the other, to teach that it is not sin, but sinful. Who will dispute the correctness of this teaching? Who would defend, as a true adherent of the Augsburg Confession, one who would teach that the nature that Christ assumed was in itself sin? There is here no addition to the doctrines of the Augsburg Confession; but only an application of one of these doctrines to a stated controversy. 2. It teaches the complete inability of unregenerate man in spiritual things, and that conversion is entirely the work of the Holy Ghost. Who that accepts Article XVIII of the Augsburg Confession can decide otherwise? Here again there is nothing but the application of a doctrine of the Augsburg Confession to a stated controversy. 3. It teaches that the righteousness which avails before God for our forgiveness, is only that which Christ wrought for us in his divinely human person, and that this righteousness is received only by faith, and that faith is not mere historical knowledge, but a divinely wrought energy in man. Can any one who has studied the Augsburg Confession detect in this any inconsistency with its doctrines? Again we have only the application of the doctrine of the Augsburg Confession to stated controversies. 4. Good works inevitably follow faith in Christ, and such an expression as that "they are injurious to salvation" should be condemned. 5. The Law convicts of sin; the Gospel alone brings grace and pardon. 6. The Law has three uses: (a) For outward discipline; (b) to convict of sin; (c) as a rule of life to the regenerate. 7. The Body and Blood of Christ are truly present with the bread and wine in the Lord's Supper, and are orally received, not in a natural, but in a supernatural and sacramental manner by all who partake, so as to strengthen the faith of even the weakest of believing communicants, and to bring judgment upon impenitent and unbelieving communicants.

8. The human nature of Christ by its union with the divine actually participates in the power and majesty of the divine nature; and although, during his humiliation, the human nature abstained from the full use of these communicated gifts, since it is exalted to the Right Hand of God, the human nature now fully exercises all that the divine imparts to it. This is only a somewhat more explicit statement of what is taught in Article III of the Augsburg Confession. 9. Christ's descent to hell belongs to his triumph. How this occurred should not be investigated; like all other mysteries, its solution should be awaited until the next world. 10. The Church of God of every time and place has the power, according to circumstances, to change its ceremonies in such manner as is most edifying; ceremonies not commanded in Holy Scripture are in themselves no part of the service of God; but in time of persecution, matters which in themselves are indifferent, may, because of their relations, become essential. This is simply a repetion and application of Article XXVI of the Augsburg Confession. 11. The doctrine concerning election must be learned not from the secret will of God, but from the Gospel, and every element included in the way of salvation taught in the Gospel enters into the decree of election. This is mentioned already in Article V. of the Augsburg Confession. 12. The last article groups together the rejection of numerous false propositions. We ask:

Is it consistent with the Augsburg Confesion, or is it not, to teach "Christ did not assume body and blood of the Virgin Mary, but brought them with him from heaven?" Is it adding to the Augsburg Confession to say plainly that such is not the teaching of those who subscribe it? Or what of the second error condemned: "Christ is not true God, but only has more gifts than any other man?" Or the third: "Our righteousness before God consists in renewal and our own godliness?" Or the fourth: "Unbaptized children are not sinners before God?" Or the fifth: "Children should not be baptized until they have attained their reason?" Some one advances the opinion: "That is no true Christian congregation wherein sinners are still found," and insists that, according to his interpretation of the Augsburg Confession, such a view is not condemned, and, therefore, he must have freedom as a Lutheran minister to proclaim it. Dare the churches which profess the Augsburg Confession be hindered from being faithful to their trust in framing an explicit declaration whereby their condemnation of such error may be known? or are they disloyal to the Augsburg Confession in so doing? Or whenever some specific error, either in doctrine or morals, arises that threatens to overthrow the faith, or at least to disturb and confuse Christian people, is it not rather the plain duty of the professed teachers of the Church to sound the note of alarm against it, even though they have to use somewhat different phraseology from that of the Church's fundamental Confession?

The General Council, by this proposition, in no way questions the Lutheran character of those who actually hold to and firmly maintain all the doctrines of Unaltered Augsburg Confession, even though they may have some difficulties concerning the policy of the ecclesiastical endorsement of the other Confessions; but, at the same time, it indicates that the only hope of abiding harmony is found, in not ignoring the experience through which the Lutheran Church has passed in maintaining the doctrines of the Augsburg Confession, but in keeping ever in mind the application of these doctrines that had to be made by the other Confessions, in order to save the Lutheran Church from hopeless discord and confusion.

In so doing it entered no new path, but followed the consistent development of Lutheran Theology, as exhibited not only in the great theologians of our Church, but especially in such earnest and well-matured practical Christians and Church-organizers as Arndt and Spener, August Hermann Francke and Henry Melchior Muhlenberg, who clearly recognized the new demands made by new issues forced upon the Lutheran Church, in the confession of the Scriptural faith of Augsburg in the ampler Confessions.

Among these issues, one of the principal arose

from the fact that the Peace of Augsburg of 1555, confirmed by the Peace of Westphalia of 1648, guaranteed to Protestants freedom of religious worship upon the sole condition of subscription to the Augsburg Confession. Repeatedly Reformed theologians and princes, who protested against the distinctive doctrines of the Lutheran Church, signed the Augsburg Confession and were allowed the rights guaranteed Lutherans, upon the plea of a general, but not of a specific agreement with it. The Confession thus lost its place as a doctrinal test among Lutherans. When the mark placed upon a house in "The Arabian Nights" was industriously copied upon all the houses in the neighborhood by enterprising boys, it ceased to be a distinguishing character. The signatures to the Confession of many who did not accept all its doctrines rendered every signature doubtful. It was for such reason that Arndt, in his dying testimony, most solemnly confessed "the true religion of the Formula of Concord," and Spener wrote an especial treatise in defence of the same Formula, and the Halle Faculty declared that they held with absolute firmness to all the Symbolical Books, and Muhlenberg challenged his accusers to find anything that he had said or written in conflict with them.

The General Council has simply placed itself unequivocally upon the foundation laid in the first Constitution of the Mother Synod, the Ministerium of Pennsylvania (ch. vi. § 2): "Every minister professes that he holds to the word of God and our Symbolical Books." The revision in 1792, after Muhlenberg's death, erased this provision, thus involving later generations in untold difficulties and dangers from doctrinal indifferentism, until a return was made to the firmer and clearer basis of the Fathers of the Lutheran Church in this country.

Following these "Principles of Faith" are those of "Church Polity." They may be briefly outlined as follows:

The power of our Lord Jesus Christ, as Supreme Head of the Church, can be delegated to no man or body of men on earth. All the power which the Church can exercise is through the administration of the Word and sacraments, and is obligatory upon its members only according to the degree in which it is faithful to Holy Scripture. The congregations are the primary bodies through which this power is normally exercised. Congregations may act through representatives in Synods, and these Synods again in a General Body. The decisions of Synods command respect, chiefly because they are presumed to be guarded by constitutional provisions, which give greater probability of correctness than those of any single congregations or individuals. They are constantly subject to revision and appeal by the congregations. Synods can deal with each other only as Synods, and the official record must be accepted as evidence of the doctrinal position. Synods are organized to maintain sound doctrine, settle controversies, regulate the externals of worship according to the New Testament, and in keeping with the liberty of the Church, and make provision for carrying on the Church's work in every department of beneficent labor.

In the "Constitution for Congregations," which claimed the attention of the General Council for a number of years, the Unaltered Augsburg Confession and the Small Catechism alone are expressly mentioned as the doctrinal standards of the congregation, while the pastor is obligated besides to the Apology, Large Catechism, Smalcald Articles and Formula of Concord. The Lay Eldership is omitted, the Deacons being, with the Pastor or Pastors, the only members of the Church Council. This provision, however, has not been universally adopted, the Lay Eldership introduced by Muhlenberg still maintaining a firm hold, especially in Pennsylvania. The Church Year and its festivals are recognized in the same document, as well as catechetical instruction, and a previous notice on the part of those desiring to partake of the Lord's Supper.

Concerning Chiliasm, the General Council declared at Pittsburg, in 1868, that "it has neither had, nor would consent to have, fellowship with any Synod which tolerates the 'Jewish opinions' condemned in the XVII Article of the Augsburg Confession."

In the same declaration it warned against "all societies for moral and religious ends which do not rest upon the supreme authority of God's Word, or recognize our Lord Jesus Christ as true God, and the only Mediator," "or which assume to themselves what God has given to His Church and its ministers," or "require undefined obligations to be assumed by oath." In the Swedish Augustana Synod, members of secret societies are excluded from the communion of the Church; in the other Synods the testimony against them is more or less pronounced, although Church discipline against them is rigidly exercised only in a few places.

Concerning "Exchange of Pulpits," the same declaration forbids the admission to our pulpits of any man, "whether of the Lutheran name or of any other, of whom there is just reason to doubt whether he will preach the pure truth of God's Word as taught in the Confession of our Church." Concerning the preaching by Lutheran ministers in other pulpits, the Pittsburgh Declaration of 1868 was reaffirmed at Philadelphia in 1885, and was rediscussed at Pittsburgh in 1889. According to it:

"Lutheran ministers may properly preach wherever there is an opening in the pulpit of other churches, unless the circumstances imply, or seem to imply, a fellowship with error or schism, or a restriction on the unreserved expression of the whole counsel of God."

The Akron Declaration of 1872 was not intended as an ample exhibition of the entire subject of Pulpit and Altar Fellowship, but simply to state certain general principles which seemed to be self-evident, making no new rule, but simply stating what was generally understood to be the practice in all our Churches.

"I. The rule is: Lutheran pulpits are for Lutheran ministers only. Lutheran altars are for Lutheran communicants only.

"II. The exceptions to the rule belong to the sphere of privilege, not of right.

"III. The determination of the exceptions is to be made in consonance with these principles by the conscientious judgment of pastors, as the cases arise."

This means that no one is to be admitted either to the pulpit or the altar, unless the Church, or its officers acting for it, are satisfied as to his fitness and preparation. The responsibility in both cases is so great that there should be no encouragement of the setting aside of the Church's provisions for guarding these two most holy places. No denial of either the Christian character or the ministerial standing of any one who would be excluded by the strict enforcement of such rule, is intended. It simply means that the Lutheran Church and no other communion is responsible for those who preach and commune in a Lutheran church. For a number of years it was a question of controversy in the General Council, whether the action at Galesburg in 1875, which declared the Rule Scriptural, abrogated or not the exceptions provided for at Akron. The General Council at Pittsburgh, in 1889, declared that the two declarations were explanatory of each other, and, therefore, that the principle of exceptions to be made by pastors as circumstances arise, still stands. The exceptions, however, must be such as carry out the spirit of the Rule.

Closely connected with this is the definition made at Lancaster, O., in 1870, of "fundamental doctrines," in which the distinction is drawn between "doctrines which are fundamental to the existence of Christianity," and those "which are fundamental to the complete integrity of Christianity." The "fundamental errorists" to be excluded from the Lord's Table are declared to be "those who wilfully, wickedly and persistently desert, in whole or in part, the Christian faith."

There has been no controversy within the General Council on the subject of election, and, therefore, no official declaration by the Council on the subject that has so largely occupied the attention of a number of the Synods. An "Opinion" was, however, published in 1884 by the Philadelphia Faculty, declaring that the terms "*intuitu fidei*," "*ex praevisa fide*" do not present a satisfactory solution of the theological problem, but that the condemnation of the use of such terms, when explained with the limitations placed upon them by our Lutheran dogmaticians, is not justified by the Confession of our Church. It is the general teaching that faith holds the same relation to election as to justification, and that, as we are justified, not on account of faith, so also we are elected not on account of faith; but that we are both elected and justified with respect to, or through the merits of Christ apprehended by faith, or with respect to or through faith apprehending the merits of Christ. Man can in no way prepare himself for divine grace, or even co-operate, by his own powers, with divine grace, when it approaches him. Faith itself is entirely the gift of God, brought to man and wrought in man, through the means of grace. Man's will is free to resist this grace at any stage. If man be saved, he is saved altogether by God's grace; if he be lost, he is lost altogether by his own sin and fault. That one accepts and another rejects divine grace, is not due to a difference made between the two by God's will. The universal grace of God is made particular by the obstinate resistance of those who repel the Holy Spirit. In those who accept divine grace, even the power to cease to resist is a special gift and endowment of the Spirit. What we call in time justification, is, with respect to the eternity that precedes time, election. God's foreknowledge of the justification of individual believers, is his election, with only this difference, that, as the will is impelled by no irresistible grace, its liability to fall continues to the end of this life, and hence justification may be only temporary; but with respect to those who remain in a justified state until the end of this life, election and justification coincide. Election is thus the pretemporal record of the justification of those who die in Christ. The entire tendency among us is to follow Luther's latter course, viz., when troubled with thoughts concerning election to find the answer by a consideration of what is involved in justification. Mysteries enough still remain, into the reasons for which we make no attempt to inquire.

The Language Question has been a prominent feature in all the discussions and work of the Council. The German, the Swedish and the English have all a good representation at all its meetings, with an occasional addition of the Norwegian. The Germans have preponderated in numbers; the English have very largely shaped its legislation and led in its debates, while the Swedes have held the balance of power. At the urgent request of the Swedes, the English has been made the official language of the Council, any one who uses another language, except from clear necessity, being in danger of a call to order from the Swedish brethren. At Chicago, in 1869, the Council declared that "it is just as possible to hold the Lutheran faith and observe Lutheran usages in the English language as in the German;" that "the pastors and people of our German and Scandinavian churches should cheerfully and conscientiously promote the transfer into English Evangelical Lutheran churches, of all those who do not understand the preaching of the Word of God in the language of their fathers," and, where there is no English Lutheran church, "encouraging the necessary steps as soon as possible for the establishment of English Mission Sunday-schools and Churches."

The General Council has always been ready to coöperate in every way, consistent with her principles, with other bodies of the Lutheran Church. She has made provision for a representation at her Sessions and participation in her debates of any Synods that adopt the "Fundamental Principles." In this way the German Synod of Iowa and former Norwegian Augustana Synod, for years, participated in the discussions, and were represented on her committees. The same is true of the Joint Synod of Ohio at her first meeting. She offered to meet any time in free conference the representatives of Synods who desired it. In 1873 she proposed to the General Synod and other bodies the holding of a colloquium, "in which all Lutherans who accept the unaltered Augsburg Confession may compare views in regard to the Confession." She entered in good faith into the movement for a Common Order of Service, and heartily coöperated in every stage of its preparation.

The Liturgical activity of the General Council

has been inherited from her oldest Synod, the Ministerium of Pennsylvania. When the General Council was formed, the English Church-Book was almost finished. It had just been published at the second session of the Council in 1868. It was very generally introduced into the town and city and many of the country churches, with some variation, however, as to the amount of the service used. Prejudice gradually vanished, and the Church-Book grew every year more and more deeply into the affections of the people, proving, wherever introduced, a powerful educator. The German *Kirchenbuch* followed. This, however, encountered more opposition, for several reasons: It was difficult to replace the familiar hymns of the Pennsylvania Synod's book by the more sober, but severely classical hymns of the new book. The opposition of Southern Germans to a full liturgical order was difficult to overcome. It has, however, been also working its way constantly towards a united use. When the "Common Order of Service" was prepared, the instructions which guided the Joint Committee being the same as those according to which the Church-Book had been compiled, led to essentially the same result, without any effort on the part of the General Council's representatives to determine it.

The New Church-Book of 1891 is the Old Church-Book, slightly modified by the Common Service revision, with the materials for Matins and

Vespers inserted, and full orders provided, according to the *consensus* of the XVI century for Ministerial Acts. Its introduction has only fairly begun; but great interest is taken by pastors, especially in the new Vesper Service. With the music of the "School and Parish Hymnal" of the Rev. J. F. Ohl, recommended by the Church-Book Committee, and that provided in "Church Song" by Dr. J. A. Seiss, as well as in the forthcoming revised and enlarged edition of "The Church Book with Music" by Mrs. Spaeth, ample material is at hand for its correct and edifying rendering. In many of the Sunday-schools, the worship has been conducted for years according to a modification of Vespers; and it is confidently expected that by this means the process of further accustoming the people to a full Lutheran Service will be accomplished. The Service is prized especially for its clear confession of the doctrines of the Church in due proportion, in regular order, and with such admirable comprehensiveness as to present throughout the year the whole counsel of God. It is of itself a creed of the people, according to the rule of St. Augustine: *Lex supplicandi est lex credendi*, giving simplest and most popular expression to the doctrines more amply stated and defended in the formal and fuller Confessions. But it is far more than a creed. The plan of salvation is not minutely dissected, as has to be done in accurate dogmatic definitions, framed for the schools, but is presented in all its simplicity and concrete reality. All its various parts center around Christ, presenting Him in all His offices, in both His states, in the fulness of His work, and in all His relations to the sinful and sorrowing, the penitent and believing, the afflicted and tempted, the dying and the glorified. Its lessons and responses and collects and chants are intended simply to carry the devotions of the worshippers to the Throne of Grace, as far as possible, in the very words of Holy Scripture. Wherever introduced it is affectionately cherished by the congregations, who could scarcely be persuaded to become accustomed to the coldness and formality and incoherency, affording little food for the heart, that so often characterizes a Service without a fixed order.

Nevertheless, our churches most devoted to the Church-Book are not so bound to the appointed lessons and prayers, as not, under peculiar and exceptional circumstances, to vary or depart from them, or even to entirely dispense with them. Where the prayers provided do not meet the circumstances of the worshippers, there is no difficulty in finding others that are suitable. Where the people are unable to use a full Lutheran Service to edification, no attempt is made to force it upon them. The general feeling is that the man is to be pitied who is so bound to a Liturgy as to be unable to find any edification except in a prayer that is read; but that he is equally to be pitied who can find no edification in the fixed prayers upon which the yearnings of the hearts of millions of God's people have ascended to Heaven for many centuries.

The General Council is only at the beginning of its work. Much time has been spent in laying the foundation broadly and deeply, and in answering questions that must be understood before a basis of widely-extended, solid and harmonious work can be reached. Her embarrassments have arisen largely from the comprehensiveness of her aims. In the endeavor to further, as far as possible, union among all Lutherans in this country, elements have been brought together at her conventions that, except for the common faith, were largely strange to one another. The very circumstances which President Bassler noted at the first convention, as indicating a remarkable Providence, have brought corresponding difficulties. He said:

"That so many persons should come together—persons who have been educated in different institutions, under diverse influences—even in different countries, and using different languages—and yet should be able to see eye to eye, so far as to use the same words in declaring their apprehension of God's Word, e. g. in the confession of their faith; and not only to use the same words, but to use these words in one and the same sense, is certainly the work of God's Holy Spirit."

But these advantages have been partially offset by the fact that it requires time to make such a body thoroughly homogeneous. Christian men must not only have the same faith, and subscribe to the same Confession, but must learn to know and understand one another by a long experience, to make due allowances for each others' faults, and to appreciate the graces of the Spirit that often abound in, and beyond, and above, the sometimes more visible works of the flesh. If the entire Lutheran Church of America is ever to be united, it will pass through the very same experience. Activity and earnestness, within one organization, of those who have been previously separated, mean discussion, delay, and sometimes even considerable friction, before a thorough understanding is reached. John Damascenus, the great theologian of the Greek Church, has well said: σύνθεσις ἀρχὴ μάχης, i. e., "Union is the beginning of controversy." The question that is often to be decided is as to whether the understanding should be reached before or after union, i. e. Shall there ever be union without unity? The General Council had no choice to make. With a sincere desire to have all Lutherans in America not only dwelling together in peace, but also vigorously prosecuting the great work opening to our Church in this country, the efforts were made to promote this end, as Providence pointed the way. Never has her harmony been greater than at present; nor is this harmony at the expense of her fidelity, or due to inactivity and indifference. But her future, like that of the entire Lutheran Church, is in God's hands; and the lot of the entire Church may be read in the career through which she has passed and is passing.

THE SYNODICAL CONFERENCE.

BY

REV. PROF. F. PIEPER.

[*Preliminary Remark.* Since the "distinctive doctrines and usages of the Synodical Conference" are based upon clearly understood general truths and principles, the author of this treatise has deemed it appropriate to introduce the presentation of the several articles here discussed by a statement of the underlying principles.]

OF THE CHURCH.

What it is. The Church, in the proper sense of the term, is *the aggregate of all true believers in Christ*. *All* those, and *only* those who believe in Christ, are members of the Church. Whoever believes in Christ, is a member of the Church, whether he be in external fellowship with an orthodox, or in external union with a heterodox congregation, or in no external connection with any church at all. On the other hand, whoever does not believe in Christ, is not a member of the Church, although he be a person of good external standing in an orthodox congregation, or even a minister or high dignitary in it. In short, *faith in Christ is the all-deciding factor in regard to church-membership.* The *wicked* and the *hypocrites*, although they have *external* fellowship with the Church, form no *part* of it. The Church is the *spiritual body* of Christ, the "congregation of *saints*," whose hearts, through faith in Christ, are ruled by the Holy Spirit, whilst all unbelievers, however holy in outward appearance, are in the power of Satan, and members of his kingdom (Eph. ii. 2).

In order to maintain the true conception of the Church, what is necessarily or commonly *connected* with it must not be confounded with the Church *itself.* For instance, *Christ* is the *head* of the Church, but not the Church *itself,* the Church being His spiritual *body* (Eph. i. 22, 23). Again, *The Word of God and the Sacraments* are necessarily connected with the Church, they being the *seed* (1 Pet. i. 23; Mark iv. 26, 27; Titus iii. 5, 6), and the *bread* (John vi. 51 compared with John viii. 31; vi. 68; 1 Cor. xii. 13), and, consequently, also the *true marks* of the Church, but they are not the Church *itself,* nor part of it. Finally, Christians dwelling together in the same place are *bound* to unite also in *external fellowship* for the purpose of preaching and hearing the Word of God, etc., and they *may* enter into a larger ecclesiastical organization with other Churches, but *no external ecclesiastical organization of any kind* is the Church itself, or part of it, the Church being "properly *nothing else* than the congregation of all believers and saints" (Augsb. Conf., Art. VIII). The Church is not a mere sum of *ordinances*, institutions, ceremonies, etc., but the great spiritual body of *men* believing in Christ.

Importance of this doctrine. It is of great importance to retain this true definition of the Church, because it may easily be shown that all errors concerning this article of the Christian faith spring from forgetting the simple truth that the Church properly *is* "*nothing* else than the congregation of believers." Moreover, by retaining this truth, we shall not content ourselves with belonging merely to the external communion of the Church, but we shall rather earnestly take heed that we belong to the internal communion of saints, and remain therein unto our end, and thus in eternity. Finally, by keeping in view that the Church is the congregation of *believers*, we shall not, for the purpose of building and extending the Church, resort to wrong means, such as temporal power, external force, human ordinances, church-fairs, church-fellowship with errorists; for by such means *faith in Christ* is neither wrought nor preserved, but, on the contrary, hindered or destroyed. Keeping in mind that the Church is the congregation of believers, we shall rather faithfully and diligently use the means ordained of God, which alone produce and preserve faith in Christ in the hearts of men, to wit, the preaching of the pure Gospel and the right administration of the Sacraments. The stress laid on the "*pure* doctrine" or "*pure* Gospel" must not be ridiculed, since the Gospel generates and preserves faith only so far as it is pure.

The Church without which there is no salvation. Of the Church which "is the great body of true believers in all parts of the world, from the rising of the sun to his setting," the proposition is true, that *there is no salvation without the Church* (extra ecclesiam nulla salus), the proposition being equivalent to what our Lord says: "He that believeth on the Son hath everlasting life; and he that believeth not the Son, shall not see life" (John iii. 36).

The Church not confined within the particular orthodox Churches or congregations. The Church without which there is no salvation, is not confined within the boundaries of the orthodox Churches, that is, of those particular Churches in which *all* the articles of the Christian faith are taught in their purity; but it is found throughout the world in those ecclesiastical communities also in which, beside errors, so much of the saving truth is taught that true faith in Christ may be produced. The so-called "Missourians," although emphasizing the distinction between orthodox and heterodox Churches, have always rejected the doctrine that the orthodox Lutheran Church is *the* Church, i. e., the Church without which there is no salvation.

This doctrine they hold to be an un-Lutheran, yea, an impious doctrine, as it overthrows the main article of the Christian religion, the article that man is justified and saved by faith in Christ, notwithstanding man's shortcomings in knowledge and life.

The Church is, and always remains, in this life invisible.

As the Church is nothing else than the congregation of believers, and God only, the searcher of hearts, knows those who truly believe, it is, and always remains, in this life *invisible*. (Luke xvii. 20; 2 Tim. ii. 19.) The Church, in the proper sense of the term, is not in part only invisible, in part, however, visible, the audible and visible means of grace constituting its "visible side." What is necessarily *connected* with the Church, is not to be confounded with the *Church itself*. Although wherever the Word of God is found, we are to find the Church, yet the Word of God forms no part of the Church, the component parts of the Church being only the *believers*. This may be illustrated by an example. Man cannot live without air and his daily bread. But the air and the daily bread do not form an essential part of *man*. So the Church lives by the Word of God, but the Word of God is not an essential part of the Church. The Church itself, therefore, can not be called visible on account of the audible and visible means of grace.

Universal Church and particular Churches.

The Scriptures not only speak of the *one* Church (Matt. xvi. 18; Eph. i, 22. 23), but frequently mention *Churches* in the plural, *e. g.*, the Churches of *Asia*, 1 Cor. xvi. 19; the Churches of *Macedonia*, 2 Cor. viii. 1; the Church of God which is at *Corinth*, 1 Cor. i. 2; the Church which was *at Jerusalem*, Acts viii. 1; "tell it unto *the Church*," Matt. xviii. 17. It is, therefore, in accordance with Scripture that we speak of *local* or *particular* Churches. But the relation existing between the particular churches and the una sancta (universal Church) ought to be rightly understood. Men cannot, like God, look into the hearts, nor should they try to do so. We, therefore, have to consider all such to belong to the particular Church as unite with us in the profession of faith and do not contradict this profession by an ungodly life. It is in this regard that the particular Churches are called *visible* Churches. But we do not on this account set up *two* Churches. For the *visible* particular Church *is* a *Church*, and is *called* a Church and has the privileges of a Church ("the power of the keys") only *on account of the true believers that are within it.* The *particular* (*i. e., local*) Churches, therefore, properly speaking, *consist* of true believers only, the hypocrites being *intermingled* with the Church through *external* fellowship solely, forming no part of the particular Church itself. This is evident from all those passages of Scripture in which the *particular* Churches are described as the "Churches of God," consisting of those "*that are sanctified in Christ Jesus*" (1 Cor. i. 2; Rom. i. 7). Hence it is, that a description of an Evangelical Lutheran local Church ("Ortsgemeinde") is given in the following words by Dr. Walther: "An Evangelical Lutheran local Church is an assembly of believing Christians in a certain place with whom the Word of God is preached in its purity, and the holy Sacraments are administered according to the Gospel." The relation between the particular Churches and the one universal Church may, therefore, be stated thus: the aggregate of the particular Churches (with the addition of those single believers who are cut off from all external Church-fellowship) is the one universal Church, embracing all true believers in all parts of the world.

ORTHODOX AND HETERODOX CHURCHES.

The particular Churches are of *two kinds*, determined by their relation to the Word of God. It is Christ's order and precept that the pure doctrine, and nothing but the pure doctrine, should be preached and heard in His Church. Throughout the whole Scriptures there is not found a single passage which authorizes or permits a minister to teach false doctrine, or a Christian to unite with those who teach false doctrine. Hence arises the difference between orthodox and heterodox Churches! A Church which conforms to the command of Christ, that is, a Church in which the Gospel is taught in its purity and the Sacraments are administered according to the Gospel, is by right called an orthodox Church; on the other hand, a Church which does not conform to the will of Christ, but allows false doctrine to be taught in its midst, is justly called a heterodox Church. As ours is an age of indifference to doctrine, Christians must take special heed that the difference between orthodox and heterodox Churches be not obliterated. And it should be distinctly understood that the character of the Churches as to their orthodoxy, is determined by the doctrine which is *actually taught*, not by the "officially acknowledged confession" kept perhaps in the archives only; for Christ commanded all the articles of the Christian faith to be taught, and not kept on record only.

The heterodox Churches are called both "Churches" and "sects" in diverse respects. They are called *Churches* in so far as, besides erroneous doctrines, essential parts of the saving truth are retained, and, consequently, true children of God may be born and are found among them; they are called *sects* in so far as they profess doctrines contrary to the Scriptures, and, by adhering to false doctrine, have caused division in the Church, and constantly imperil the faith and salvation of the children of God.

What position Christians ought to maintain toward the existing heterodox Churches.

As no person is licensed to speak aught but the Word of God in the Church (1 Pet. iv. 11), and no Christian is allowed to unite with a teacher who in any way deviates from the doctrine revealed in Holy Scripture, Christians who are not yet connected with heterodox Churches, should *avoid* them, and Christians already united with them, should *come out* from among them. It is not according to the *good pleasure* of God—as modern theologians teach —that sects exist, for all Christians are required to agree on all articles of faith revealed in Holy Scripture (1 Cor. i. 10; Eph. iv. 3-6), but sects arose and exist by God's *forbearance* only, like other sins. Sects arise and continue, not for the purpose that Christians should *join* them, but for the purpose that Christians should prove their allegiance to God by *avoiding* them, as the Scriptures explicitly teach, 1 Cor. xi. 19: "There must be also heresies among you, that they which are approved may be made manifest among you."

To unite with heterodox Churches, must not be *excused* by pointing to the fact that many dear children of God are found among them. As it was not lawful for the Israelites to join with Absalom, although two hundred men out of Jerusalem went with the rebel "in their simplicity" (2 Sam. xv. 11), even so it is not lawful for Christians to unite with those ecclesiastical communities that rebel against Christ by proclaiming false doctrines, although many Christians "in their simplicity" and by mistake have joined them.

Here the question may be answered what position a Christian should hold in regard to the so-called FOUR POINTS.

Chiliasm. By chiliasm we understand the doctrine according to which a glorified state of the Church on earth in a millennial reign is to be expected. It is a *false* doctrine, as it contradicts several clearly revealed truths, especially the truth that the Church on earth is to be a kingdom subject to the cross even unto the end of the world. (Acts xiv. 22; Luke xviii. 8.) It is, besides, a very *dangerous* doctrine, as it perverts the hope of the Christains, inviting them to hope for a glorification in this world, instead of in the world to come. Consequently, chiliasm must not be treated as an "open question," but every Christian, every congregation, and every ecclesiastical body, are bound to *reject* the chiliastic opinion.

Pulpit-fellowship. All Christians are commanded to *avoid* those who teach doctrines contrary to the Scriptures (Rom. xvi. 17); teachers, therefore, who in any way proclaim false doctrines, are not to be *admitted* into, but to be *excluded* from our pulpits. As this rule is taken from the Word of God, it admits of no exception, but applies to every case and occasion. The practice of pulpit-fellowship with errorists cannot be excused on the plea of its being demanded by *love*. For it is contrary to both the love toward *God* who bids us "*avoid*" false teachers and not to *invite* them into our pulpits, and the love toward our fellow-men, as it is our Christian duty to warn them against error, and not to confirm them in it. Moreover, it is patent that by the practice of "exchanging pulpits" the dissensions in the Church, caused by false teachers, are not removed, but continued and ratified.

Altar-fellowship. In regard to altar-fellowship the same reasons hold good which forbid Church-fellowship with errorists. Altar-fellowship certainly is Church-fellowship. There is, however, an additional reason to be noted on this point. According to the explicit statement of Holy Scripture all such as are not able to "discern the Lord's body," partake unworthily of the Lord's Supper. Consequently, love bars us from admitting to our altars Christians who do not believe the real and substantial presence of the body and blood of Christ in the Holy Supper, and, therefore, are not able to discern the body of the Lord. This rule too, being taken from the Word of God, admits of no exceptions. To say that making exceptions should be left to the discretion of the individual pastor or congregation, is, in fact, granting a license to act against the Word of God. Suspension of altar-fellowship is not to be called excommunication. The Lutheran Church denied altar-and pulpit-fellowship to the Reformed, without denying that there are Christians among the Reformed.

Secret societies. Secret societies, such as Odd Fellows, Free Masons, etc., are incompatible with the Christian Church. For in these societies a way is commended *of obtaining* "*eternal happiness,*" not through Christ, however, and Him crucified, but by "moral education." There is *praying* also in the Lodges, but not in the name of Jesus Christ. From this it appears—not to mention the ungodly oaths and other objectionable features connected with membership in the Lodges—that a Christian can not enter into membership with secret societies without professing a false way to heaven and participating in a false worship, and thus denying Christ, man's only hope for salvation. It is the sacred duty of the Christian Church to raise her voice against secret societies, for a public testimony; and especially for the purpose of regaining such of her members as are already led astray by the Lodges.

OF THE MINISTERIAL OFFICE.

The ministerial office, that is, the office of the preaching of the Word and the administration of the Sacraments, is not of human ordinance, but of *divine* institution.

As it is God who instituted the ministerial office, so it is *He* who calls certain persons to this office, Acts xx. 28; Eph. iv. 8, 11, 12; Matt. ix. 38. Thus far all parties agree.

But *through* whom, i. e., what human agency, does God effect his call? Here, disagreement begins. The right answer is: The right and power of electing and calling ministers of the divine Word is *primarily and immediately* granted, not to the pope, nor to bishops, nor to the ministry, nor to a Consistory, nor to the Presbytery, nor to a civil power of any form, but to those to whom *all* spiritual power ("Church-power") originally and immediately belongs, namely, the *congregation of believers.* As it is the congregation of believers that has the keys of the kingdom of heaven, (Matt. xvi, 19, xviii. 18), that is primarily commissioned to teach all nations and to administer the Sacraments, (Matt. xxviii. 19, 20), that is the "royal priesthood" for showing forth the praises of him who hath called them out of darkness into his marvelous light, so it is, in the very nature of the case, the congregation of believers that is entrusted with the power of appointing ministers. Hence, the Lutheran Church confesses in the Smalcald Articles: "Where there is a true Church, there must be the right to elect and ordain ministers." No human authority can remove this right from the congregation of believers, as it was granted to them by Christ when they became children of God through faith in Christ, and is, consequently, inhering in their being Christians. The congregation of believers may, of course, transfer the *exercise* of this right to one or more persons. Ministers called by individual persons or a body of persons in the name of the congregation of believers have received a valid and divine call. But it ever remains true and must never be forgotten, that the only body to whom the right and power of calling ministers is *originally* entrusted, is the congregation of believers. Whoever is called to the ministerial office by this body either directly or indirectly, has received a *divine* call; whoever derives from other sources the authority to teach publicly, is to be classed with those of whom the Lord says: "I have not sent these prophets, yet they ran" (Jer. xxiii. 21). All this may be summed up thus: the ministerial office is conferred by God upon certain persons through the divinely prescribed call of the congregation, the congregation being, by the gift of Christ, the original possessor of all Church-power. The ministers have their office from Christ, not immediately, however, but mediately, by the Church, in virtue of delegation through the call. According to Holy Scripture the members of the Christian Church among themselves constitute a spiritual *republic* (Matt. xxiii. 8). As the office of a Governor or President in a republic is not a personal prerogative of an individual person or order of persons, but the common property of the whole free and sovereign nation, which delegates its right to the office through election to a certain person: even so the ministerial office and all spiritual rights are the common property of the free and sovereign people of believers

(Matt. xxiii. 8; 1 Pet. ii. 9,) who delegate the divinely instituted office of the ministry through the divinely prescribed call to certain suitable persons. The ministers are not only servants of *Christ* (1 Cor. iv. 1), but also servants of the *Church* (2 Cor. iv. 5), performing the functions of the office in the place and name of the Church, and being accountable for the faithful discharge of their duties not only to Christ, but also to the congregation (1 Colossians iv. 17.)

The proper answer to the question whether it is the *udiversal* or the *local* Church that is entrusted with the right of calling ministers, is that Christ clearly ascribes "the keys of the kingdom," and, consequently, the right to appoint ministers, to the *local* Church. For it is the local Church which Christ addresses when He says: "Whatsoever ye shall bind on earth, shall be bound in heaven; and whatsoever ye shall loose on earth, shall be loosed in heaven." "For where two or three are gathered together in my name, there am I in the midst of them," Matt. xviii. 18, 20.

Ordination. It is the *call* of the congregation that constitutes ministers, and actually confers the ministerial office. *Ordination* is not a *divine* ordinance, but an *apostolic-ecclesiastical institution.* It does not confer the ministry, as Papists and Romanizing Protestants assert, but is only a public testimony and confirmation of the call. Ordination, therefore, is not essential to the validity of the ministerial office.

The right of judging on questions of doctrine does not rest with the Church at large only, nor with Synods only representing the Church of a certain country, nor with the clergy alone, but *with all individual Christians,* since upon all Christians is laid the duty of distinguishing pure teachers from deceivers, and of departing from error, Matt. vii. 15; Rom. xvi. 17. To take away from Christians the right of judging on questions of doctrine, is an abominable outrage, and the origin of popery.

Obedience is due to the ministerial office, whenever it sets forth the Word of God. Beyond these limits obedience must neither be *demanded* nor *rendered.* A minister who demands obedience of Christians in things not commanded or forbidden by the Word of God, puts himself in the place of Christ, for it is Christ's privilege to be the Master of those who believe in Him (Matt. xxiii. 8). A Christian who allows men to bind his conscience beyond the Word of God, by this very fact and in this regard falls away from Christ as his only Master, and becomes an idolator, paying divine honors to mortal man. It is a misuse of the Fourth Commandment when ministers in demanding obedience in things not commanded by God refer to that Commandment. What is true concerning ministers, holds good also in regard to the socalled representative Church, namely, in regard to Synods, Church Councils, etc. If the decisions and injunctions of the "Church" are identical with the

Word of God, they are to be obeyed, not because they are the decisions of the *Church*, but on account of their being the very Word of God. If they go beyond these limits, either by declaring to be true what the Scriptures pronounce to be false, or by making obligatory upon the consciences of Christians what is a matter of indifference, all Christians are bound to disregard them. There is absolutely no authority in the Church beyond the Word of God, and there is, consequently, no authority on earth that could make the least thing, not prescribed by Christ, obligatory upon a Christian's conscience. The pope, says Luther, has the power of laying a fast upon *himself*, but not on some second person in the whole world. This holds true concerning all matters of indifference and with all persons.

But as there are, within the individual congregations, many things to be determined upon which Christ did not prescribe, how then are these things to be arranged? Not by the clergy alone commanding the Christian people what to do, nor by the majority prescribing conscience-binding laws to the minority, nor by some authority outside of the congregation deciding for the congregation what was left undecided by Christ, but by the deliberations and the mutual agreement of the whole congregation, the minority submitting to the majority, or the majority to the minority, "for the sake of charity and tranquillity," as the case and occasion may require. Matters of indifference are easily arranged if the Christians do not walk after the flesh, but after the Spirit. When they walk after the flesh, they will try to lord over their brethren; when they walk after the Spirit, they are always ready to submit to them for charity's sake.

Synods must not claim divine authority over the congregations connected with them, but carefully keep within the sphere of *advisory* bodies. The local congregation is the highest divinely instituted tribunal in the Church, as is seen from Matt. xviii. 17. All jurisdiction exercised over congregations by persons outside of the congregations is of *human* ordinance only.

OF CHURCH-UNION.

All *Christians* are already *one* in Christ. Christ's promise that "there shall be one fold and one shepherd" (John x. 16), has been in the course of fulfillment ever since the times of the apostles, whenever a soul by true conversion was added to the communion of believers. All Christians actually agree on the main article of Christian religion, namely, on the article that they have forgiveness of their sins through faith in Christ alone, and not by their own works, although many of them are in external connection with heterodox churches, and, by infirmity, err in some parts of doctrine. For it is this faith that makes a man a

Christian and unites him with the spiritual body of Christ.

Nevertheless, it is a deplorable state of things, that there are external Christian communities differing in doctrine. Sects, as stated before, do not exist according to God's will and good pleasure, but only by God's forbearance. All Christians, therefore, should be desirous of a reunion, and earnestly labor for the same.

But the union sought for must not be a so-called organic union only, but a union in faith and doctrine. Christians may differ and, in many cases, owing to different circumstances, must differ as to ceremonies, external organization, etc. But there is one thing concerning which all Christians of all times and of all countries should perfectly agree— they should be one in *faith and doctrine*. "I beseech you, brethren," St. Paul says, "by the name of our Lord Jesus Christ, that ye all speak the same thing, and that there be no divisions among you, but that ye be perfectly joined together in the same mind and in the same judgment" (1 Cor. i. 10).

How is this union to be effected? Sects arose when certain persons taught contrary to the Scriptures, and others, instead of rebuking their errors, united with them. The only way, therefore, to cause the divisions to disappear, is to remind the Christians of their duty to part with error, and, consequently, with all persons that persist in proclaiming doctrines contrary to Holy Scripture, and to unite with those that teach the pure word of God. Christians should never agree to disagree on any article of faith, but earnestly endeavor to bring about an agreement on all doctrines revealed in Holy Scripture. Nothing but the revealed truth, and the *whole* revealed truth—that is the platform which God has made for the Christian, and which every Christian is commanded to stand upon. An agreement on a more or less comprehensive collection of so-called "fundamental articles," selected by man, leaving a portion of the divinely revealed truth to the discretion of the dissenting parties, is a position wholly unbecoming to Christians, for, not to deny, but to confess the Word of Christ, is their duty in this world.

But is perfect agreement concerning doctrine *possible?* We most emphatically answer: it is, as the Scriptures are perfectly clear on all articles of faith, every article of faith being revealed at least somewhere in the Scriptures in plain and proper words. God, by graciously giving his Word to men, did not propose to them a collection of riddles, but made his word to be "a lamp unto our feet, and a light unto our path" (Ps. cxix. 105), "a light that shineth in a dark place" (2 Peter i. 19), "making wise the simple" (Ps. xix. 7). Erring concerning any article of faith is impossible as long as the words of Scripture are retained as they read. Ere falling into error is possible, the plain words of Scripture must have either been entirely set aside or twisted from their natural meaning according to human reason or feelings.

ON "OPEN QUESTIONS."

There are, indeed, "open questions" if this term is used in the sense of "theological problems." Such are all those questions which are not decided in Holy Scripture. Open questions in this sense are never to be "closed," since no human authority, be it called "Church" or otherwise, can supply the lacking decision of Holy Scripture. This would be "adding unto the Word of God" and denying that the written Word of God is the only rule and standard of faith and life. Theologians should not waste their time and energy in trying to solve questions not answered by the Bible. On the other hand, all doctrines revealed in Holy Scripture are to be accepted and believed, for the very reason that they are propounded in Holy Scripture, no matter whether "decided" in the Symbolical Books and agreed upon by the theologians or not. To declare doctrines revealed in the Bible to be "open" or "free" for the reason that they are not yet "symbolically fixed" in the Confessions of the orthodox Church, or not yet accepted by all orthodox theologians, would, in fact, be the same as to put the Church, her Confessions and theologians, in the place of Holy Scripture, and to ascribe to the Church and her theologians the authority of establishing articles of faith. We, of course, insist upon accepting the Confessions of the Lutheran Church without exception and reserve, as we are convinced that *all* doctrines propounded by them (either "ex professo" or incidentally) are in strict accordance with Holy Scripture, and we, moreover, maintain that a qualified acceptance of the Confessions of the Lutheran Church makes a qualified Lutheran. But we, nevertheless, denounce any position as un-Lutheran according to which the Confessions are to take the place of the Scriptures.

ON SUNDAY.

Sunday in the New Testament is not instituted by *God*, as was the Sabbath in the Old Testament; yea, Sabbath, or any other day, as a divine institution, is clearly abolished in the New Testament, as St. Paul declares: "Let no man therefore judge you in meat, or in drink, or in respect of a holyday, or of the new moon, or of the Sabbath days" (Colossians ii. 16). Hence we are not bound by any law of *God* to observe either Sunday or any other day. Sunday belongs to the *Church* ordinances, and is to be classed with Christmas, Easter, Pentecost, and other Christian holy days. The Christian Church has, in the free use of her liberty, chosen Sunday for a day of divine worship, because some time or other must be selected for hearing the public preaching of the Word of God.

We do not oppose *Sunday laws* enacted on merely *social* reasons; for public welfare demands a day of rest from daily labor "that both man and beast might be refreshed, and not exhausted by constant labor." But every Christian is in conscience bound to oppose all Sunday laws based on the assumption that Sunday is of *divine* ordinance, for by lending support to this assumption, we would participate of *false* doctrine and entangle Christians again with the yoke of bondage wherefrom Christ hath made them free. In the Augsburg Confession the "Sunday question" is summed up thus: "Those who are of opinion, that the ordinance of Sunday instead of the Sabbath was established as a thing necessary, err very much. For the Holy Scripture has abolished the Sabbath, and teaches, that all ceremonies of the old law, since the revelation of the Gospel, may be discontinued. And yet as it was necessary to appoint a certain day, so that the people might know when they should assemble, the Christian Church ordained Sunday for that purpose, and possessed rather more inclination and willingness for this alteration, in order that the people might have an example of *Christian liberty*, that they might know that neither the observance of the Sabbath, nor of any other day, is necessary." The "Sunday question" is not an "open" one, but clearly decided by the Word of God.

ANTICHRIST.

Holy Scripture speaks of "*many* antichrists" (1 John ii. 18). As Christ alone is to rule in his Church by his Word, all false teachers setting forth in the Church their own doctrine instead of Christ's set themselves against Christ, attempt to cast off the authority of Christ and to overthrow his kingdom. Hence all false teachers are justly called antichrists. But the Scriptures speak also of *one* Antichrist in whom the principles and spirit of the many antichrists are to culminate. This Antichrist, commonly called the *great* Antichrist and graphically described in the second chapter of the second epistle to the Thessalonians, we believe to be the pope at Rome, the papacy.

To this doctrine, so clearly stated in the Confessions of the Lutheran Church and once generally accepted by all Lutherans, exception is taken now. Modern Lutheran theologians, although acknowledging antichristian traits in the papacy, are waiting for a still greater foe of the Christian Church. But it is from ignorance or from a lack of due consideration as to what the Christian Church really is, when the pope at Rome is not recognized as the greatest possible human foe of the Christian Church, and when worldly potentates like Napoleon, or even Boulanger, are thought of as the Antichrist. The Christian Church is the communion of believers, that is, of those who believe that they are justified and saved by confiding in Christ's merit alone and not in any merits of their own. It is this faith that constitutes the very essence of the spiritual life of a Christian. What the water is for the fish and the air for bodily life, that is reliance on God's grace in Christ alone for the spiritual life of the Christian. As soon as this faith is enkindled in their hearts they become Christians, as long as this faith continues in them they remain Christians, and the very moment this faith is extinguished in them, they cease to be Christians. Who, therefore, is the greatest enemy of the Christians or the Christian Church? He who uses every means to destroy in the hearts of Christians the faith that relies on Christ's merit alone. But this is what Rome is engaged in. Rome not only rejects the doctrine of justification through faith in Christ alone, but she, in the Resolutions of the Council of Trent, *curses* this truth by which Christians live. And she not merely curses it, but the whole system and machinery of Romanism has the tendency to hinder and destroy faith in Christ and to engender trust in man's own works. It was, indeed, a fearful thing when men like Nero slaughtered thousands of Christians. But it was a small affair when compared with what Rome does. For Rome incessantly takes the spiritual life of millions of Christians by taking from them faith in Christ as the only Mediator between God and man, not to mention here that Rome also drank the blood of the martyrs of Jesus whenever she had the power to do so.

Again, Christians are to be ruled by Christ's word alone (John viii. 31), Christ claiming the prerogative to be their only Master (Matt. xxiii. 8). But the Pope at Rome, under the pretense of being Christ's vicar on earth, alters and annuls Christ's Word and Commandments at his pleasure, bearing himself as if he were a God on earth.

And this dreadful and blasphemous work Rome does under the disguise of exquisite holiness. The infidels, of course, blaspheme Christ too, but they do it openly, and all Christians know that they have to beware of them. Rome, however, rejects and blasphemes Christ under the outward appearance of Christianity, and under the claim of being the Church without which there is no salvation, sustaining this false claim by all manner of deceits, by signs, and by lying wonders. Thus the papacy is the greatest possible foe of Christ and His Church, and all the traits which in 2 Thess. ii. are ascribed to the Antichrist, that he is to arise in the Church, exalting himself above all human authority, assuming to himself the prerogative of God, and sustaining these assumptions "with all power and signs and lying wonders"—all these traits we find in the pope at Rome. Hence, we fully and heartily indorse the doctrine of the Lutheran Confessions, that the pope is the great Antichrist of whom Scripture has prophesied. In the papacy we see the great Antichrist standing barely and squarely in the sight of the Christians and doing his fearful work, and, therefore, we are not looking forward to any other great Antichrist to come in future times.

We do not, of course, hold, as we are frequently represented, that this doctrine of the Antichrist is a fundamental article of the Christian religion. For man is saved by knowing Christ, not by knowing and recognizing Antichrist. But what we hold is this: every Christian, knowing Christ well, will recognize the papacy to be the very Antichrist, as soon as he becomes thoroughly acquainted with the teachings and doings of Rome. Especially we hold those *theologians* to be rather poor theologians who, knowing the doctrine and practice of the papacy, fail to recognize it to be the true Antichrist.

ON ABSOLUTION.

Absolution is nothing else than the *Gospel* directed to one or more individual persons who desire it. By the word of absolution the forgiveness of sin is really *offered* to all who hear it, and actually *conferred* on all who receive it in faith.

It is for a two-fold reason that to many Christians the practice of absolution is a matter of great offense. In the first place, they confound the divinely instituted absolution (John xx. 23; Matt. xviii. 18; xvi. 19) with the Romish caricature of such institution. According to the Romanists, absolution is an act which only the Roman priest can perform, and by which the priest sits in judgment on the sinner, pardoning and condemning at his discretion. This doctrine, indeed, is as blasphemous as it is ridiculous, but it has nothing in common with the biblical doctrine held by the Lutheran Church. According to Holy Scripture, absolution is not a power vested in the ministry or any certain order of persons, but a power granted to the whole Church, i. e., to all believers. This is clearly seen by comparing John xx. 23, Matt. xvi. 19, with Matt. xviii. 18. In fact, all Christians when they console one another with the Gospel, they actually absolve. A child pronouncing the words of the Gospel remits sin just as effectually as a bishop, minister, etc.

But the main reason why so many Christians take offense at the practice of absolution is to be found in their inadequate ideas as to what the Gospel of Christ properly is. Their conceptions of the *vicarious work of Christ*, and consequently of the *Gospel* also, fail to come up to the biblical standard. They think that Christ has only brought about so much for us that *we* now, by our conversion, faith, and prayers, render God fully propitious, and thus obtain forgiveness of sins. Hence, they conceive the Gospel to be the declaration of certain *conditions* on which God would forgive sin. With many Christians and teachers the Gospel is a mere *plan* to save sinners, Christ having caused in the heart of God a certain *tendency* to forgive sin, men *completing* the change in the heart of God by their being sorry for their sins, by their praying to God for forgiveness, by their earnest endeavors to lead a better life, etc. But these conceptions both of the work of Christ and the Gospel are altogether wrong. Christ has already perfectly and completely reconciled the whole world unto God, and the Gospel, being the message of what Christ has done for mankind, is "the Word of reconciliation," viz.: the word stating that God *is* reconciled—*perfectly* and *completely* reconciled—through Christ to the whole world and every individual sinner. The Gospel is not the Word which teaches how *men* might by their own exertions render God fully propitious, but the Word which assures us that God *was* reconciled to all men through the vicarious sacrifice of Christ. Therefore, to preach the Gospel does not mean to lay before men a mere *plan* of salvation, or to declare the *conditions* of forgiveness, but preaching the Gospel is preaching pardon itself, salvation itself, "remission of sins" itself (Luke xxiv. 47). The Gospel is "nothing else than a great letter of pardon directed to the whole world." Hence it is that Luther frequently says: "A minister preaching the Gospel can not open his mouth without constantly remitting sin." Wherever the Gospel is proclaimed, there absolution is pronounced. *It is from this conception of the Gospel that the Lutheran practice of absolution is to be judged and understood.* It should be borne in mind also that God has already *absolved* the whole world in laying the sins of the whole world on Christ and in raising up Christ from the dead. With *our* sins upon him Christ entered into the prison-house of death; absolved from *our* sins he was set free in his resurrection. Hence it is seen that the resurrection of Christ actually involves an absolution of the whole world, and the absolution we pronounce is nothing but a repetition or echo of what God has long since pronounced.

But what of the necessity of *faith?* Faith, indeed, is necessary on the part of man; not, however, to render God fully propitious, or in any way to merit forgiveness of sin, but to *accept* of the forgiveness already earned by Christ and now offered in the Gospel. "Absolution"—says Dr. Walther—"demands faith, and faith alone receives what is offered and given by it; neither absolution, nor any means of grace, operates ex opere operato."

It is of great importance to maintain this true conception of the Gospel, viz., that forgiveness of sins exists for every sinner before his conversion and faith. For, how could man obtain forgiveness of sin *by faith*, *i. e.*, by *laying hold on it* by faith, if this forgiveness did not actually exist for him in Christ and were not offered to him in the Gospel?

To this doctrine is objected: "The forgiveness of sin is the prerogative of God." This is true! Whoever is not absolved by *God*, remains under the burden of sin, although he be a thousand times absolved by men. But now the question arises whether God absolves *immediately*, e. g., by visible apparition, or *mediately*, by using certain means. We most emphatically deny the former and affirm the latter. God performs his absolution *through the Word of reconciliation.* And this Word of reconciliation he has not kept for himself, but committed *to his Church* on earth. St. Paul after having stated "that God was in Christ reconciling the world unto himself, not imputing their trespasses unto them," immediately adds: "and hath committed unto *us* the word of reconciliation." This, therefore, is the state of things: Christ having committed to His Church the *Gospel*, thereby committed to her the right and enjoined upon her the duty of forgiving sin. No one who concedes the former can consistently deny the latter. Hence, Christ in describing the agency by which sin is forgiven (John xx., Matt. xviii., Matt. xvi.), names the congregation of believers: "Whatsoever *ye* shall loose on earth shall be loosed in heaven," and "Whosoever sins *ye* remit, they are remitted unto them." What is true of the preaching of the Gospel, is true also of the administration of the Sacraments, the Sacraments being nothing but the "*visible* Gospel." The person administering the Sacraments is, in fact, administering absolution. The person saying "I baptize you," at the same time says "I absolve you." Baptism is a private absolution. So is also the Lord's Supper.

Against absolution, moreover, is objected: "It is impossible to believe that God has given men the power of forgiving sin, unless he has given them the power of infallible judgment." This objection rests on the false supposition that absolution is a decision rendered on the state of man's heart, while it is a declaration given on the state of *God's* heart, namely, that God *is* reconciled to every sinner through Christ. God being perfectly reconciled to every sinner through Christ, as Holy Scripture reveals, no infallibility whatever is required on the part of man to pronounce absolution, but only a mouth to give utterance of a fact clearly revealed in Holy Scripture. Absolution is founded on two facts, first, that God is perfectly reconciled through Christ to every sinner; secondly, that God has commanded this Gospel to be preached in the world, and especially to the penitent sinners who long for the consolation of the Gospel. Absolution *demands* faith on the part of man, yet it is not *based* upon faith, but pronounced for the purpose of being *appropriated* by faith.

From the Lutheran Confessions the following statement concerning absolution may be cited here: The power of the keys announces to us the *Gospel*, through absolution; for absolution proclaims peace to the soul, and is *the Gospel itself.* . . . When we hear absolution, that is, *the promise of divine grace*, or the *Gospel*, our hearts and consciences are consoled. Inasmuch as God truly grants new life and comfort to our hearts *through the Word*, our sins are truly remitted here on earth through the power of the keys, so that we are released from them before God in heaven; as we find, Luke x. 16: "He that heareth you, heareth me." We should, therefore, esteem and believe the words of absolution no less than the clear voice of God from heaven. (Apology, N. M. ed. p. 236.)

OF JUSTIFICATION.

By justification we understand the remission of sins. Since Christ has already perfectly *acquired* forgiveness of sins for all men, and since this forgiveness is offered and exhibited to men through the means of grace, to wit, the Gospel and the Sacraments: the *only* means on our part of obtaining forgiveness of sins and salvation is that *faith* which accepts of the promise of God. All works and worthiness of our own are entirely excluded as a means of obtaining remission of sins or justification.

This is the *main* article of the Christian religion. It is by this article that the Christian religion is *distinguished* from all other so-called religions. There are *only two* essentially different religions in the world. According to one, justification and salvation is obtained, either totally or partially, by man's own works; according to the other, justification and salvation is obtained without works by faith, that is, by merely accepting of the grace of

God in Christ, exhibited in the Gospel. The latter is the Christian religion, the former the heathen religion in its various forms.

From this it appears that by corrupting the article of justification the essential feature of the Christian religion is destroyed. This is done e. g. by *synergism*. The assertion, that conversion and salvation depends not only upon the grace of God but to some extent also on the conduct of man, overthrows the article of justification, destroys the essential character of the Christian religion, and places it on equal footing with the heathen religions.

OF CONVERSION.

As natural man is *dead* in sin (Eph. ii. 1), yea *enmity* against God (Rom. viii. 7), his coming to God or his conversion is solely the work of God who through the means of his Word produces a new spiritual life and creates a new willing heart. The Scriptures explicitly declare that man's conversion is accomplished by the same *infinite* power by which God created natural light out of darkness (2 Cor. iv. 6), and raised Christ from the dead (Eph. i. 19, 20).

Hence there is no *co-operation* whatever on the part of man towards his conversion, but man is only the *object* that is to be converted. There are not *three*, but only *two* causes of conversion: The Holy Spirit and the Word of God; by adding a *third* cause, to wit, the will of man, or by asserting that conversion depends not only on divine grace, but to some extent also on man's conduct, synergistic error is taught.

The converting or regenerating grace, however, is not *irresistible*. Man can offer *resistance* to God's earnest, regenerating grace, and thus *prevent* conversion, as Holy Scripture clearly teaches (Acts vii. 51; Matt. xxiii. 37). But man can not *promote* his conversion. He is not able to refrain from resisting the grace; non-resistance must be effected by the Holy Spirit. From man's ability to "behave evil" towards the Gospel (Matt. xxiii. 37) his ability to refrain from resistance, or to "behave well" toward converting grace must not be inferred (1 Cor. ii. 14). Hence it is rightly said *non-conversion* depends upon man's *evil conduct*, but it is not in accordance with the Scriptures to say that *conversion* also depends on man's *good conduct*. Hodge (Systematic Theology ii. 649) entirely misstates the Lutheran doctrine when he says: According to the Lutherans, "the fact that one man is converted under the call of the Gospel and not another, that one accepts and another rejects the offered mercy, is to be referred solely to the fact that one does, and the other does not resist that influence." Lutherans who are in accordance with the Lutheran Confessions will say: The fact that one man is converted under the call of the Gospel, is to be referred solely to the grace of God, non-resisting not being antecedent but consequent to the operation of grace. The fact, however, that another man is not converted, is to be referred solely to man's voluntary resistance (Formula of Concord, S. D., XI. §§ 57–64, p. 716).

To this position the following objection is urged: If conversion is exclusively the effect of divine grace, or if conversion depends upon grace only and in no way on man's "conduct," "self-determination," etc., then God appears to pass by some men with his converting or regenerating grace. We hold fast, however, that a converted person is such only by the grace of God; while on the contrary, an unconverted person is such by his own fault, because he wantonly resists the grace of God. We have here before us a great mystery. We, of course, know of *two* ways by which we might explain away this mystery. We might have recourse to an absolute decree of reprobation and say: God's converting grace is not *universal;* consequently only some men are converted. But this way of solving the mystery—the *Calvinistic* way—is contrary to the Scriptures (1 Tim. ii. 4; Acts xiii. 46; vii. 51); hence we can not make use of it. Or we might say: conversion does not depend upon grace alone, but to some extent also on man's conduct, self-determination, etc., and this is the reason why not all men are converted. But as this way of explaining the mystery—the *synergistic* way—is also at war with the clear statements of Scripture, we leave the mystery unsolved, hoping for a solution in the world to come. In the meantime we abide by the Word of God spoken through Hosea: "O Israel, thou hast destroyed *thyself*; but *in me* is thine help" (Hosea xiii. 9).

OF PREDESTINATION.

The distinguishing feature of our doctrine concerning predestination or election may be briefly stated thus: We differ from all those who in any way limit either *universal* or *free* grace.

There is no predestination to death. As to universal grace we teach that God's earnest, sincere, and efficacious grace extends to all men alike, in such a manner, that all those who remain unbelievers, remain such solely by their own fault. We, therefore, *reject* the distinction between *common* grace and *efficacious* (regenerating) grace, the former extending to all men, the latter being granted to the elect only. For the grace granted to those who remain unbelievers and against which the unbelievers harden themselves, Holy Scripture clearly describes as sincere and efficacious grace (Acts xiii. 46; Matt. xxiii. 37; Acts vii. 51). Even those passages of Scripture that treat of *obduration* inflicted by God on some persons, do not prove that God passed them by, but rather that He visited these with his saving grace, for obduration is represented by Holy Scripture as a punishment for *contemning* and *resisting* the grace of God. Yea, according to Scripture, some of those who are actually lost, enjoy even a more abundant measure of grace than some of those who are actually saved (Matt. xii. 41). We teach and confess that damnation comes upon men not for want of grace on the part of God, but for contempt of grace on the part of men (Acts xiii. 46; Matt. xi. 25). There are, indeed, some historical facts (e. g., that many nations are destitute of the preaching of the Gospel) which present a seeming contradiction to the universality of grace. But we deem Holy Scripture to be clearer than history. In spite of all *seeming* contradictions, we abide by the clear statements of the Scripture asserting God's earnest, sincere, and efficacious grace to be universal (1 Tim. ii. 4; Ez. xxxiii. 11). There is no predestination to unbelief and damnation.

There is a predestination to salvation. Holy Scripture, although utterly silent on a predestination to death, clearly teaches a predestination to *salvation*, pertaining not to all men, but only to those who are actually saved. Holy Scripture clearly reveals the fact that all those who are actually converted, preserved in faith, and saved, by the divinely established common way of salvation, are *from eternity* in God's counsel elected and predestined to be saved in this way and in this order, Eph. i. 3–6; 2 Thess. ii. 13, 14. "The eternal election or predestination of God"—the Formula of Concord says—"that is, the ordaining of God unto salvation, does not pertain both to the good and the bad, but only to the children of God, who were elected and ordained to eternal life, before the foundation of the world, as Paul, Eph. i. 4, 5, declares: "He hath chosen us in Christ Jesus, and predestinated us unto the adoption of children."

Causes of eternal election. God elected those who are elected solely out of His *mercy* and on account of *Christ's merit* earned for all. Election has not taken place on account of *anything good*, even not on account of *faith*, which God foresaw in the elect. According to the universal Christian order of salvation, all those who are actually converted and saved, are indebted for their conversion and salvation to God's free grace in Christ, their conversion and salvation being in no way secured or promoted by anything good found in themselves. Even so their *eternal election* to conversion and salvation is not dependent on or conditioned by anything good found in themselves, be it called "good works," or "good conduct," or "self-determination," etc., but eternal election solely flows from God's *free grace* in Christ. This doctrine, and none other, is revealed in Holy Scripture. Holy Scripture not only teaches that God has chosen us *in Christ, according to the good pleasure of his will, to the praise of the glory of his grace* (Eph. i. 4–6), but expressly denies that there be a cause of election *in man;* "not according to our works, but according to his own purpose and grace, which was given us in Christ Jesus before the world began" (2 Tim. i. 9; John xv. 16.) In this sense St. Paul calls election "the election of *grace*," adding for the purpose of explanation as to what "grace" is: "and if by grace, then is it no more of works; otherwise grace is no more grace" (Rom. xi. 5, 6). The Lutheran Church confesses concerning the causes of election: "The following doctrine is *false and erroneous*, namely, that not the mercy of God alone, and the most holy merit of Christ are the cause, but that *in us also* there is a cause of the election of God, on account of which God has elected us to everlasting life." This is Lutheran doctrine! The doctrine that God elected on account of foreseen "good conduct," "self-determination," "non-resistance," etc., we hold to be both un-Lutheran and unchristian, denying free grace, and thus falsifying the Christian way of salvation.

Relation of eternal election to the faith of the elect. In the decree of eternal predestination the *faith* of the elect is not *presupposed* (as is assumed by the theory that predestination took place "in foresight of faith)," but *included.* For God did not first elect them to salvation absolutely, and *after that* decree to grant them faith as the means of obtaining salvation, but when God elected them He at the same time and in the same decree decreed to grant them faith and perseverance in faith. As God *in time* unites His children to himself by giving them faith, so *in eternity* he united His children to himself by decreeing to give them faith. The very substance of eternal election consists in this, that God decreed to grant his children faith in Christ and preserve them therein. "God took" —the Formula of Concord says—"so deep an interest in the conversion, righteousness, and salvation of each Christian, and so faithfully provided for these, that before the foundation of the world, in His counsel and purpose, He ordained the manner in which He would bring me to salvation, and preserve me there." If, therefore, the question be asked whether the faith that is found in the elect in time, in the order of thought precedes their eternal election as a cause, condition, etc., or follows after it as a result, the latter must be affirmed and the former denied. For in all passages of Scripture treating of this matter, not only faith, but the entire state of grace with all the spiritual blessings bestowed upon the Christians in time, are represented as *flowing from* their eternal election, Eph. i. 3–5: "Blessed be the God and Father of our Lord Jesus Christ, who blessed us with all spiritual blessings in heavenly places in Christ: *According as he hath chosen us* in him before the foundation of the world, that we should be *holy* and without blame before him in love: Having predestinated us *unto the adoption of children*" etc., Acts xiii. 48: "as many as were ordained to eternal life believed. See: 2 Tim. i. 9; 2 Thes. ii. 13, 14; Rom. viii.

28–39. Hence the Formula of Concord states: "The eternal election of God not only foresees and foreknows the salvation of the elect, but through his gracious will and good pleasure *in Christ Jesus*, is also the *cause* which procures, works, facilitates, and promotes our salvation and whatever pertains to it." And it is this relation of the eternal election to their faith and continuance in faith that the Christians find such a precious *consolation* in the doctrine of election, as the Formula of Concord puts it: "This doctrine also affords the eminent and precious consolation, that God took so deep an interest in the conversion, righteousness, and salvation of each Christian, and so faithfully provided for these, that before the foundation of the world, in His counsel and purpose, He ordained the manner in which He would bring me to salvation, and preserve me there; again, that he wished to secure my salvation so truly and firmly, that in his eternal purpose, which cannot fail or be overthrown, he decreed it, and to secure it, placed it in the omnipotent hands of our Saviour, Jesus Christ, out of which none shall pluck us, John x. 28. For, if our salvation were committed unto us, it might easily be lost through the weakness and wickedness of our flesh, or be taken and plucked out of our hands, by the fraud and power of the devil and of the world."

OBJECTION TO THIS DOCTRINE.

To this doctrine the following objection is made by Calvinists: To affirm an election to salvation, and to deny an election to death, is an "illogical" position, according to the rules of human reason. We reply that we are well aware of this, and, morever, that we know all the means employed both by Calvinists and Synergists, to remedy this "inconsistency." But this illogical position is that of the Scripture. Holy Scripture clearly teaches a predestination to salvation, which is a cause of the conversion and salvation of the elect; but it does not mention a preterition or predestination to death, which is a cause of the unbelief and damnation of those who perish. This is clearly seen from Acts xiii, 48 compared with v. 46. Verse 48 we hear of *believing Gentiles*, and their faith is referred to their eternal election: "As many as were ordained to eternal life believed." Verse 46 we hear of *unbelieving Jews*, but their unbelief is not referred to an eternal predestination to unbelief and death, or to a lack of grace on the part of God, but solely to the Jews' wilful resistance to God's sincere and efficacious grace; for Paul and Barnabas address the Jews thus: "Seeing ye put it (the Word of God) from you, and judge yourself unworthy of everlasting life, lo, we turn to the Gentiles." It is sound theology to speak where Scripture speaks, and to be silent where Scripture is silent.

The Synergists urge the objection: If you insist upon the grace of God and the merit of Christ as being the only causes of eternal election, denying that election was also on account of man's foreseen "good conduct," "self-determination," etc., you will be forced to admit that God's sincere and efficacious grace is not universal. This conclusion, however, we do not admit, since Scripture does not admit it. Holy Scripture, in revealing God's eternal election, never makes it dependent on man's "good conduct," etc., but merely on God's free grace in Christ. Scripture at the same time maintains the universality of grace. And so do we, maintaining unimpared both *free* and *universal* grace.

But finally our doctrine, *to wit*, that election "is also the *cause* which procures and promotes our salvation and whatever pertains to it," is charged with introducing a *twofold* way of salvation, the way of *grace* pertaining to all men, and the way of *election* pertaining to those only who are actually saved. In answering this objection, we might simply refer to Holy Scripture, which plainly asserts election to be a cause of the salvation of the elect. But by duly considering the matter it is easily understood that we do not introduce *two* ways of salvation, but maintain the *one* universal way of grace in regard to the elect also. For it is one and the same efficacious, saving grace by which the children of God are saved, and against which the children of unbelief harden themselves. And as the children of God during this life are brought to conversion, justification, sanctification, etc., *out of pure, free grace* in Christ without any merits of their own, even so they are *from eternity elected* to salvation and whatever pertains to it, not in consideration of any good conduct found with them, but *out of mere grace* in Christ. Hence the one way of grace is not destroyed by this doctrine, but rather *confirmed* by it, as the Formula of Concord expressly remarks: "It *confirms* most forcibly the article, that we are justified and saved by *pure grace* for the sake of Christ alone, without any of our works and merit." But when it is affirmed that conversion and salvation do not depend on grace only, but to some extent on man's conduct also, and, consequently, that *eternal election* also took place in consideration or foresight of this conduct of man, then, indeed, the one old Christian way of salvation is entirely abandoned and a new way of salvation is introduced, altogether different from the revealed way of grace.

The mystery to be acknowledged in this doctrine. There are some things in this doctrine which we know, and there are others which we know not. We exactly know the reason why those who are actually saved, are elected, brought to faith and preserved in it. It is, so Scripture clearly reveals, out of God's pure, free mercy in Christ. We also know the reason why those who perish are not converted or not preserved in faith, and thus go to perdition. It is, as Scripture likewise plainly teaches, from their own fault, namely, from their obstinate resistance to the saving grace of God. But we do not know the reason why one person *in preference to another* is converted and saved, *as all men by nature are equally guilty and dead in sin.* By acknowledging a mystery right here we must not be charged with *Cryptocalvinism. For this and none other* is the doctrinal position of the *Lutheran* Church. The Formula of Concord stating the case thus: "that God gives his Word to one region, but not to another; or that one man is hardened, blinded, and given over to a reprobate mind, but that another, though equally guilty, is converted to God," refers us to Rom. xi. 33, 34: "O the depth both of the wisdom and knowledge of God! how unsearchable are his judgments, and his ways past finding out! For who has known the mind of the Lord?" The same position is, as with one voice, avowed by the great Lutheran theologians of the sixteenth century. *Martin Chemnitz e. g.*, writes thus: "Our Catechism, in the third article of our Christian faith, says that by his own reason or strength man cannot believe in, or come to Jesus Christ, but that the Holy Ghost must bring him to such faith, *for faith is a gift of God; how, then, is it that God does not bestow such faith upon the heart of Judas, so that he also could have believed* that Christ could help him? *Here we must restrain our questions* and say (Rom. xi.): 'O the depth of the riches both of the wisdom and knowledge of God! how unsearchable are His judgments, and His ways past finding out!' *We are neither able, nor bidden to search this out*, and must not be absorbed in such thoughts." The mystery which the Lutheran Church acknowledges at this point may only be solved either by denying with the Calvinists God's *universal* grace, or by denying with the Synergists God's *free* grace, as was shown before.

As to the dogmatical phrase (which was introduced into the Lutheran Church by *Aegidius Hunnius*) that election has taken place "in view of faith," we hold, in the first place, that it is not taken from the Holy Scriptures. In the passage Rom. viii. 29: "whom he did foreknow, he also did predestinate," *foreknow* does not denote the simple foreknowledge of God—for thus a universal election would result, as God's simple foreknowledge extends to all men—but foreknow here is used in the sense of, "to appropriate, to make his own beforehand," as *know* and *foreknow* are used in other passages of Scripture, e. g., Amos iii. 2: "You only —O children of Israel—have I *known* of all the families of the earth." See Rom. xi. 2; Gal. iv. 9; Ps. i. 6. Hence the Formula of Concord paraphrases Rom. viii. 29, 30, thus: "Whom He did *predestinate, elect and ordain*, them He also called." In the second place, we hold, that the phrase "in view of faith" is not found in the Lutheran Confessions; in the third place, that it does not solve the mystery, if at the same time the biblical doctrine be maintained that faith is a free gift of grace, and in no respect man's own work; in the fourth place that, if the phrase "in view of faith" be exchanged for "in view of man's *conduct*," "in view of man's *self-decision*," etc., the mystery, indeed, is solved, but by the key of *synergism*. The *Lutheran* grounds are entirely abandoned. For the Lutheran Church confesses: "The following doctrine is false and erroneous, namely, that not the mercy of God alone, and the most holy merit of Christ are the cause, but that *in us also* there is a cause of the election of God, on account of which God has elected unto everlasting life."

Assurance of election. That a believing Christian can become and be certain of his eternal election, is a matter of course with Holy Scripture, for Holy Scripture uses eternal election as a means to comfort the Christians in their temptations and tribulations; for instance, Rom. viii. 33: "Who shall lay anything to the charge of God's elect?" As to the quality or character of certainty, it is best described as a certainty of *faith*, for it results, not from searching into the secret counsel of God, nor from hearing the law and its comminations, but by attending to and believing *the Gospel of Christ*, in whom eternal election has taken place in eternity and is now revealed in time.

THE UNITED SYNOD IN THE SOUTH.

BY

REV. EDWARD T. HORN, D. D.

THE name *The United Synod of the Evangelical Lutheran Church in the South* is a territorial designation. The other great divisions of the Lutheran Church in this country are marked by doctrinal or historical peculiarities; the General Synod, for instance, by the limitation of its confession to the Augsburg Confession and its endeavor to comprehend on that basis all variations on minor points of belief, and also by the fact, in relation to other bodies, that it is a predominantly English body. The General Council, occupying almost the same territory as the General Synod, embraces German Synods and English and Scandinavian, and acknowledges certain fundamental principles which confess the whole body of Symbolical Books as well as definite principles of church government. The Joint Synod of Ohio again is based upon the Symbolical Books, and is clearly united upon certain inferences from them, and is to be found in parts of the same territory with the bodies just named. And the Synodical Conference, besides the acceptance of the Book of Concord and the assertion of what are called the "Four Points," has clearly stated its doctrine of the government of the Church, is bound together by a peculiar history, and is predominantly a German body. THE UNITED SYNOD IN THE SOUTH embraces: 1. Certain Synods which formerly belonged to the General Synod, but were separated from it by the war, and which at the close of the war found the Synods they formerly were associated with divided between the General Council and the General Synod, while they themselves had begun a development of their own; 2. Certain Synods formed since that separation; and 3. Synods that never had been in the General Synod, but even from the first had maintained an opposition to it.

It is a territorial designation. With the exception of a couple of German congregations in Richmond, Va., which are independent or belong to the Missouri Synod, and a few in North Carolina or Virginia, which have broken from her Synods and joined the Joint Synod of Ohio, and an independent German Church in Atlanta, Ga., *the United Synod in the South* embraces all the Lutheran congregations in Virginia, North Carolina, Georgia, Mississippi and Florida and those of Eastern Tennessee. It does not include the whole South, for there is a German Synod in Texas connected with the General Council, and certain mission posts of the Missouri Synod in New Orleans and along the Mississippi. But the Georgia Synod has congregations in Alabama, and the Tennessee Synod has missions in the same state.

It would be interesting to note the characteristics of these Churches. One familiar with them would be able to show that each Synod represents a distinct community; but another would find a strong family likeness between all the Lutherans of the South. At a meeting of the United Synod the delegates from the Virginia and Georgia Synods are not unlike; and those of the Synods which for a long time were separated and opposed to each other, are of the same looks and tone.

At Winchester, Woodstock, Newmarket, Va., in the region of Salisbury and Concord, N. C., in Orangeburg, Lexington, Newberry, Charleston, S. C., we find churches of the first generation of Lutherans in America. The Salzburgers of Effingham Co., Ga., with their ancient settlement, venerable church edifice, graveyard, communion plate, records, date from 1734. The Church at Savannah is later. Salem, Va., Wilmington, N. C., Columbia, S. C., Augusta, Ga., and the Holston Synod of East Tennessee represent a later activity; and Roanoke, Va., Richmond, Charlotte, Knoxville and churches in Florida, belong to the more recent extension of the Church.

The South is an agricultural community. So the vast majority of the Lutherans in the South are farmers. Their homes are plain. Their living is frugal. They live far apart. They handle little money. Their congregations are small and not wealthy. They are of independent mind. And because of wide separation from one another, they are likely to be as much moved by the sentiment of the community in which they dwell, as by the common opinion of their coreligionists far away. They are of German descent and exhibit the traits of their ancestors. But there are only a few German congregations among them, and these are in cities recruited by later immigration, and therefore not in complete sympathy with the descendants of an earlier immigration, nor able to exert upon the latter the wholesome influence of a devotion to the traditions of the German Church. If their means and their own peculiar vocation be taken into account, it will be found that the Southern Churches have not lagged; though the progress of the Church in the South has to take its own direction and go at its own rate, and not all methods are applicable here which elsewhere have proved useful.

This is not the place to detail the history of the plantation of the Lutheran Church in the South; nor to show how it was brought within the attractions of the general system by that remarkable man Henry Melchior Muhlenberg; nor to recite the wonderful achievements of the travelling preachers sent out by the Mother Synod of Pennsylvania. These belong to the common history of the Lutherans in America. But it is necessary to show the two lines of development whose convergence has resulted in the *United Synod in the South.*

It is noteworthy that the progress of every Lutheran body in this country has been marked by an increasing appreciation of the Confessions contained in the BOOK OF CONCORD. The General Synod (of the Evangelical Lutheran Church in the Confederate States of America, afterwards *in North America*) was organized at Concord, N. C., in 1863, by delegates of the Synods of Virginia, Southwest Virginia, North Carolina, South Carolina and Georgia. The *doctrinal basis* then adopted was:

> 1. We receive and hold that the Old and New Testaments are the Word of God, and the only infallible rule of faith and practice.
>
> 2. We likewise hold that *the Apostles' Creed*, *the Nicene Creed*, and *the Augsburg Confession*, contain the fundamental doctrines of the Sacred Scriptures, and we receive and adopt them as the exponents of our faith.
>
> 3. Inasmuch as there has always been, and still is, a difference of construction among us with regard to several articles of the Augsburg Confession; therefore we, acting in conformity with the spirit and time-honored usage of our Church, hereby affirm that we allow the full and free exercise of private judgment in regard to those articles.

The *minutes* say that "the *third* section, defining the doctrinal basis of this Synod, elicited an animated, free, yet fraternal discussion—each member conscious of a great responsibility, solicitous of establishing such a platform as would secure the future unity of the Lutheran Church in the Confederate States, and without burdening any one's conscience in reference to the doctrinal symbols of the Church. After the unanimous concurrence of the brethren on the article by all rising to their feet on giving their votes, the venerable president, Dr. Bachman, invited the whole Synod to unite in returning thanks to the Lord for such an expression of harmony on the most important part of the Synod's business."

In 1867 the General Synod resolved

"That we feel bound as an ecclesiastical body to withhold our *imprimatur* from any religious publication, of whatever form, which shall inculcate principles opposed to the doctrine of the Augsburg Confession as construed and defended by our Church in her symbolical writings.

"That we feel in like manner bound to appoint or employ no professor in our theological schools who shall teach doctrines at variance with our time-honored confession."

These resolutions were offered by a committee consisting of Rev. Drs. Rude, D. F. Bittle and Dosh. And the "Revised Constitution" printed in the first edition of the Book of Worship omitted "*the third section*" altogether.

In 1872 the General Synod adopted a paper written by Dr. Dosh, in which it declared that, "It has placed itself unequivocally upon the

Œcumenical Creeds and the Augsburg Confession in its true native and original sense." "As a consequence the entire Church within its limits has become more fully identified in sympathy and opinion with the doctrines of the Reformation by Luther and his co-workers." The constitution of the Theological Seminary, printed with the Minutes of 1873, requires the Professors to acknowledge the Canonical Books of the Old and New Testaments as the only Rule of Faith, the three General Creeds, as exhibiting the faith of the Church universal in accordance with this rule, and the Augsburg Confession, as in all its parts in harmony with the Rule of Faith and a correct exhibition of the doctrines of the Word of God. The *Book of Worship*, published in 1868, contained the doctrinal Articles of the Augsburg Confession and Luther's Catechism, and in the Ordination Service required the candidate to swear fidelity to the Word of God and to the Confessions of our Lutheran Church founded thereon; and its Confirmation Service asked a pledge of life-long fidelity to the Confessions of the Evangelical Lutheran Church.

There has been a continual progress in knowledge of these Confessions and perception of their accordance with the Scriptures. They were studied for the most part in the Newmarket translation of the Henkels; and at a later period in Jacobs. The ministers in the South have meagre salaries and cannot buy many books. As a consequence, they study those they have, thoroughly. And there are few parsonages in which will not be found the BOOK OF CONCORD and SCHMID'S DOGMATICS, both filled with markers and carefully annotated. One esteemed pastor who has ministered to a venerable community for forty years, told me that he had for himself traced each position of our Confessions through the whole Scriptures; and after such study, pursued for years, had got complete conviction of the identity of the body of truth the former confess, with the Word of God. Even laymen have been known to carry the *Book of Concord* with them to their work, to read and study in it at the nooning or after work was done. The result of such faithful investigation was shown when the North Carolina Synod, which for a while had stood by itself, approached the General Synod in 1880, "To inquire into the doctrinal position of that body with a view to an organic union with it." The General Synod then said "of the Symbols adopted subsequently to the Augsburg Confession as a further defense of the truth of God's infallible Word,"

"We acknowledge said additional testimonies as in accord with and an unfolding of the teachings of the Unaltered Augsburg Confession; or in the exact language of the Formula of Concord concerning them, and the Augsburg Confession as well, that they have not the authority of a judge, for this honor belongs to Sacred Scriptures alone; but that they only bear witness to our holy faith, and explain and exhibit in what manner in every age the Holy Scriptures were understood and set forth in all articles contested in the Church of God by teachers who then lived."

Finally, in 1882, the General Synod declared that she was ready to co-operate with other Lutheran bodies towards organic union "on an unequivocal Lutheran basis." She had thus come, in the process of her own proper growth, to an unreserved and sincere adoption of all the Confessions of the Lutheran Church.

Meanwhile, it must be said that while the practical endeavors of the General Synod South were not fruitless, they brought a succession of disappointments. To the end of its history, it had not effected any great missionary work. The South Carolina Synod had maintained a Theological Seminary since 1832, in which Dr. Ernest Hazelius had been a teacher; and later, for a little while, Dr. James A. Brown; and with which at different times Revs. L. Eichelberger, Dr. A. R. Rude and Dr. J. P. Smeltzer were connected; and from which came out many useful and devoted men, to whose fitness and industry are due the preservation and extension of the Churches in the southernmost states. In 1872 this Seminary (having been transferred to the General Synod in 1867), was removed to Salem, Va., and Rev. S. A. Repass, D. D., was elected *South Carolina Professor.* A second professor (Rev. T. W. Dosh. D. D.,) was not added until 1878. The Synods did not seem hearty in their support of the Seminary, and, though a good many recognized the service it was doing, it was summarily closed by a majority of one vote by the General Synod at Charleston in 1884, and the resignation of the professors was accepted. The South Carolina Synod thereupon reopened the Theological Seminary in connection with Newberry College.

A Church paper had been begun with the new organization and after many vicissitudes survives in the *Lutheran Visitor*, which, though of no little use in holding the Synods to common work, is now in private hands. The project of a Publication Society, although often revived, has fallen through.

It always has been difficult to consolidate the union of the Southern synods and to concentrate their energies. They are far apart, and separated by long stretches of country in which are none of our faith; each Synod is weak, and each has much to do on its own territory; local prejudice is strong; there does not seem to be money enough for the administrative expenses of central boards and general secretaries; and the circulation of newspapers and appeals for aid published by the General Synod North and the General Council, the visits of Northern Secretaries, and the division of sentiment caused by the incoming of ministers trained in the rival schools of the North, while it never has availed to destroy the conviction that the Lutheran Church in the South has a peculiar character and a duty of her own, has distracted the attention of our people from their own work, made them discontented with their own small performance, and threatened to introduce divisions and quarrels with which we ought to have nothing at all to do.

The abiding work of the General Synod South is the BOOK OF WORSHIP, of which we will speak hereafter.

But the *United Synod of the South* embraces more than the former "General Synod in North America." Besides these are the Tennessee and Holston Synods; the latter an offshoot of the former, organized in 1861. At its very organization in 1820 the Tennessee Synod adopted the Augsburg Confession and Luther's Small Catechism as its doctrinal basis, and was distinguished by its bold and intelligent defense of the distinctive doctrines of the Lutheran Church. This was at a time when other Lutheran bodies in America had declined from the Confessions of the fathers. In 1866, in its revised constitution, this confessional statement was enlarged to include all the confessions of the Book of Concord:

"It receives also the other Symbolical Books of the Evangelical Lutheran Church, viz., the Apology, the Smalcald Articles, the Smaller and Larger Catechisms of Luther, and the Formula of Concord—as true Scriptural developments of the doctrines taught in the Augsburg Confession.

This Synod was peculiarly active in the translation and dissemination of these confessional writings. The Henkels of Newmarket, Va., published the Augsburg Confession and the Catechism in English and German; a translation of the whole Book of Concord in 1851; a revision of the same in 1854; and a translation of Luther's Sermons on the Epistles in 1869. The ministers of the Tennessee Synod, trained as they have been for the most part in the homes and companionship of older ministers, have not a wide and varied culture, but possess a profound acquaintance with the writings of Luther and a ready and genial knowledge of the Holy Scriptures.

At the beginning of its history the Tennessee Synod set itself against the organization of the (old) General Synod. Among the most prominent advocates of that movement, was a member of the North Carolina Synod who was a minister in the Moravian Church, and at that time the same Synod ordained a minister for the Protestant Episcopal Church. It will not be denied that at the time of the organization of the General Synod, the importance of sound doctrine was not recognized, and the Lutheran Confessions were not known and studied as they should have been. It may not be known that while the advocates of closer association dreamed of an eventual organization of all the Christians in the United States, their original project for a General Synod proposed to recognize the ordination of no Lutheran minister without its express sanction. The Tennessee Synod therefore opposed it as a sanctuary of lax doctrine and spiritual tyranny. The champions of opposing views became involved in further controversy, in misunderstanding, in encroachments upon each other; until Lutheran Synods occupying the same territory began to look upon each other as the worst enemies. As a result, the Tennesseans held aloof from all the general movements which at an earlier period have done so much good, such as the American Sunday-school Union, the Bible Society, etc., and fell into the danger of disregarding even the good objects of these organizations, because of objectionable principles allowed by them. For a while the strength of the Tennessee Synod was given to the maintenance of Orthodoxy; nor are we able to deny that their championship was needed and has been effectual. But a reaction set in. The true faith began to glow with loving sympathy with brethren at work for the Lord; it became dissatisfied and threatened to languish in isolation and inactivity. So, at the same time, the other Synods of the South reached the conviction of the substantial solidarity of all the Lutheran Confessions, and owning these as their own convictions of the truth, saw that the Tennesseeans were their brethren; the Tennesseeans recognized their orthodoxy in turn, and were desirous to help in those works which heretofore these had essayed in vain.

In 1883 propositions were laid before the Synods

composing the General Synod looking to a new union which should embrace the Tennessee and Holston Synods also. The Virginia Synod took the lead in approving this, and laid down a course for itself which the other synods adopted. The General Synod at Charleston, in 1884, resolved to take up the matter and appointed commissioners to represent each Synod in a Diet or Free Conference with the representatives of the two Synods. The General Synod was careful to assert its own devotion to the Lutheran confessions and the soundness of its past history, but professed itself willing to make any right sacrifices for the sake of ultimate union. This action of the General Synod was approved by all the Synods except that of Georgia, but its delegate also was present at the meeting of a Diet at Salisbury, N. C., November 12, 13, 1884, though he protested that he came only as a Commissioner of the General Synod. A "Basis of Union," said to have been substantially the work of Rev. Socrates Henkel, D. D., approved by Rev. J. Hawkins, D. D., was considered in committee, amended, and ultimately adopted. The "Confessional Basis" as finally adopted is that of the Tennessee Synod, and reads as follows:

'The Doctrinal Basis of this organization shall be,
"1. The Holy Scriptures, the Inspired writings of the Old and New Testaments, the only standard of doctrine and Church discipline.
"2. As a true and faithful exhibition of the doctrines of the

Holy Scriptures in regard to matters of faith and practice, the three Ancient Symbols, the Apostolic, the Nicene and the Athanasian Creeds, and the Unaltered Augsburg Confession of Faith; also, the other Symbolical Books of the Evangelical Lutheran Church, viz.: The Apology, the Smalcald Articles, the Smaller and Larger Catechisms of Luther, and the Formula of Concord, consisting of the Epitome and Full Declaration, as they are set forth, defined and published in the Christian Book of Concord, or the Symbolical Books of the Lutheran Church, published in the year 1580 (see the Epitome, *of the Compendious Rule and Standard*, and the *Solida Declaratio, Preface*, as true and Scriptural developments of the doctrines taught in the Augsburg Confession, and in the perfect harmony of one and the same pure, Scriptural faith."

The first draft presented to the Diet was rejected, because it did not preserve the singular pre-eminence of the Augsburg Confession; and that the manner of the acceptance of these Confessions may not be misunderstood, references to their own declarations are added with a final explanatory clause derived from the "Fundamental Principles" of the General Council. The substance of the declarations referred to may be given in the following paragraphs:

"The distinction between the Holy Scriptures of the Old and New Testaments and all other writings is preserved, and the Holy Scriptures alone remain the only judge, rule and standard, according to which, as the only touchstone, all dogmas must be discerned and judged, as to whether they be good or evil, right or wrong.

"We have only meant that we have a unanimously-received, definite, common form of doctrine, which our Evangelical Churches, together and in common, confess; from and according to which, because it has been derived from God's word, all other writings should be judged and adjusted as to how far they are to be approved and accepted."

Thus the Confessions of our Church again proved to be a Christian Book of Concord.

A constitution was yet to be adopted, if a real organic union was to be made. The same committee was appointed to report a constitution, and before it a complete draft was laid. This, besides other provisions which the delegates might not be prepared to adopt, contained a distinct enactment of what have been called in our Church "the Four Points," viz., the prohibition of Pulpit and Altar Fellowship with those who are not of our Church, of Membership in Secret Societies, and of "Chiliasm." This draft was laid aside; and as the *Basis of Union* already adopted seemed to present the whole compass of the consent of all the Synods, and also expressly limited the functions of the general body to be "only of an advisory and recommendatory character in all matters, except such as pertain to the general interests or operations of the Church;" the Basis itself was made the outline of a Constitution, whose omissions were filled up from the old Constitution of the General Synod. This was adopted with but three votes of dissent, as I remember it; two declaring their agreement with the President of the meeting, Rev. P. C. Henkel, D. D., "who approved the Constitution so far as it goes; but declined to vote for it because it is silent in regard to Pulpit and Altar Fellowship, Secret Societies and Chiliasm." Dr. Polycarp Henkel has since been called out of the strife of tongues into the peace of God.

In June, 1886, the General Synod held its last session, at Roanoke, Va., and at the same time a Diet assembled. The General Synod formally closed up its affairs; the Diet heard the favorable reports of the Synods on the Basis and Constitution adopted at Salisbury; and the *United Synod in the South* was organized; the General Synod formally merging itself into it and transferring to it all its possessions, works and undertakings; a trust which the United Synod as formerly accepted.

Thus the 18,000 Lutherans who formally had been a General Synod, and the 14,000 of the Holston and Tennessee Synods, struck hands and began to work together to fulfil a common duty. There is little difference between them. And yet, having been long apart, and having inherited distrust and hostility, and having for a long time supported and been recruited by separate teachers and schools, it could not be expected that questions should not rise to disturb this consummation.

It can be said of the doctrinal basis of the Southern Synods that it is the sincere and intelligent Confession of the Churches. By this I do not mean that the Lutheran Churches in the South have pondered all the controversies in which the

Symbols originated and to which they gave the answer; nor that they have accepted all the inferences which sincere Lutherans now draw from the Confessions and even may be justified in urging. But it is true that no teacher is acceptable among us who rejects any of these Confessions, or of whose sincere belief of them and thorough knowledge of them we have any doubt. The Holy Scriptures are our only rule of faith, and we know no better guide into their sense than these Confessions afford, and we perceive their exact accordance with the rule of faith, and as we study them we rejoice in the consciousness of the entire conformity of our faith with that of the fathers and confessors of our Church. In controversy it is usual to appeal to them; and all our teachers regard their word as final in decision of what is Lutheran doctrine and Lutheran practice. It has been thought by some that to subscribe Articles of Faith, to be sworn upon the Confessions of the Church as our candidates for ordination are, might limit freedom of investigation and lay a burden on conscience; but it is not too much to hold that the Southern Churches as a whole receive the Symbolical Books, and especially the Augsburg Confession and the Small Catechism, with which they are most familiar, because they believe them; and they believe them because they set forth the Word of God. The time may indeed come—though may God in His mercy forbid it—when our Churches shall decline from this faith; but rather do we hope and pray that all our brethren may come to this assurance of faith, and be of one mind with us and with one another.

Before we proceed to the later and not untroubled history of the United Synod, it will be interesting to note what the General Synod turned over to the new body. First, was an organized *Board of Missions and Church Extension*, which at that time was receiving and disbursing money for a Foreign Mission in connection with that of the General Synod North, at Guntur in India. This mission came to an end because of the unexpected resignation of the missionary. In 1888 it was resolved to attempt a mission in Japan. The first missionary sailed in February, 1892, and another in the following autumn. The Board has been more successful in Home Missions. The income has gradually increased; a Secretary is employed, who has general supervision; a monthly devoted to *Mission News* is published at Augusta, Ga., under his direction; the church at Augusta, Ga., (materially helped by the South Carolina Synod); a church at Knoxville, Tenn., with other missions in East Tennessee, with the churches at Richmond, Va., and another at Winston, N. C., receive its care. In this work the Board has been upheld by the Women's Missionary Societies Each Synod has its own Synodical Women's Society, and they coöperate under the direction of the Board. Besides this general work, the Church Extension Society and Women's Society of the S. W. Va. Synod, and also the Church Extension Society of the Virginia Synod, have done prompt and successful work in the new manufacturing towns in their own states. In 1883 a *Service and Hymns for Sunday-schools* was published, which maintains a very high standard of sacred poetry and sacred music, and essays to teach the children the requisites of the service of the Church. Of this, nearly 3,000 copies have been sold. The General Synod also transferred the copyright of *the Book of Worship* and the manuscript of the *Common Service*, which the United Synod at its first convention adopted and ordered to be published as soon as possible.

One of the first acts of the General Synod of the South on its organization had been the compilation and publication of a BOOK OF WORSHIP for its churches, which at that time was the completest book of the sort in the English language for Lutheran congregations. It contained no distinct Evening Service; the Morning Service and the Communion Office were modeled on that presented in a Provisional Service of the Pennsylvania Synod; and it was affected by some peculiarities of the Danish Liturgy. It did not contain the Collects; and had only ten Introits for the Sundays; but for each of the Great Festivals had a special Introit and a Festival Prayer. The service began with an Introit; the Confession of Sins followed; and after it was the Kyrie. The Ten Commandments might be substituted for the Creed. The book contained the Litany, the *Te Deum* and the Passion History. After the Hymns a series of prayers for private and family devotions was given, from the "old New York Hymn Book." The Doctrinal Articles of the Augsburg Confession and Luther's Small Catechism, together with the three Œcumenical Creeds, were printed in a separate part. Before the Passion History, the Penitential Psalms were given. The Book contains also a complete series of Orders for Ministerial Acts, which for the most part are based on those of the Pennsylvania Synod.

This book found immediate acceptance among the more intelligent members of the Southern churches. By the time of the union at Roanoke, at least 10,000 copies were in use. No Synod or Conference sanctioned any other order of worship. The Book of Worship secured substantial uniformity in the use of a dignified and historical liturgy in nearly all the churches of the General Synod.

Meanwhile, the General Synod was engaged in a continual effort to amend and improve the book. Every successive edition showed the removal of typographical errors and the improvement of rubrical directions. In 1876 committees were appointed to revise the various parts of the book; and at that meeting the Committee was instructed "to confer with the Evangelical Lutheran General Synod in the United States and the Evangelical

Lutheran General Council in America with regard to the feasibility of adopting but one book, containing the same hymns and the same order of services and liturgic forms, to be used in the public worship of God in all the English-speaking Evangelical Lutheran Churches in the United States." This was the beginning of the movement to secure a Common Service. It had been suggested in 1870, in a letter from the venerable Dr. Bachman to the General Synod, but the time was not then ripe. The matter was brought up again in 1878, and steps were taken to urge the Northern bodies to a definite reply. At the same meeting the Committee was enlarged and the object of the continuous amendment of the Service was declared to be "the ultimate attainment of the distinctively Lutheran cultus, breathing the spirit of our Evangelical faith, and which is a legitimate outgrowth therefrom, and at the same time is in full accord with the service of the Primitive Church." In 1882 the General Synod referred to this Committee many proposed changes, and in 1884 adopted a long series of them; so that, if the *Common Service* had not finally been adopted, the Southern Book of Worship, in its new edition, would have contained the Introits and Collects for the Church Year, the prescription of the Epistles and Gospels, of the Nicene Creed and of the Proper Prefaces in the Communion Service. The determination was asserted "to prosecute the revision of the Book of Worship in honest fidelity to the spirit and history of the Lutheran Church, in order that, at all events, we may possess a ritual as nearly correct as it can be made." In 1886 the Protocol of the Joint Committee outlining the *Common Service* was presented and approved.

The accession of the Tennessee and Holston Synods did not take from the liturgical spirit and zeal of the Southern churches. Before, they had used in many of their churches the *Church Book*, published by the General Council in 1868; based, like the Book of Worship, on the Provisional Service of the Pennsylvania Synod, and representing a liturgical progress which culminated in the *Common Service*. Accordingly the outline of the Common Service was adopted by the United Synod immediately on its organization, and in 1888, the complete MS. was laid before it and approved.

On the publication of the Common Service in 1888, it met with an immediate welcome in all the Southern Synods. The principles which underlay it and the successive stages in its preparation had been laid before the Church and pondered by it. It was introduced into all the leading churches, and its use is enjoined by some Synods. It gives order to our worship, secures uniformity among us, provides a system of devotion in harmony with our faith, maintains among us the fundamental doctrines of God's Word and an administration of the sacraments according to the Gospel, and stores in the minds of our children the form of sound words; and while we rejoice in our accord with the fathers of our own church and with the Church of all ages in the use of these venerable forms, the Southern Church has hoped to fulfill her own special vocation in uniting in this the churches of the General Synod and those of the General Council with her own. This hope seems destined to fulfillment; and already the English churches of the Synod of Missouri and of the Joint Synod of Ohio are adopting this Common Service of the Lutheran Church.

But though the adoption of a common service of worship was thus attained, new questions arose, which have threatened the union which seemed so necessary to the advancement of our Church in the South. When the Salisbury *Basis of Union* was reported to the Tennessee Synod it was adopted, but the following was added:

"In adopting this, as the Evangelical Lutheran Tennessee Synod rejects all ecclesiastical union and co-operation which is not based on the pure Lutheran teaching and faith; as the Exchange of Pulpits, Promiscuous Communion or Altar Fellowship, Secret Society Worship and Chiliasm, we, the ministers and lay-delegates, in Synod assembled, do hereby recommend or advise the Committee, or the Chairman of the Committee, appointed by the United Synod of the Evangelical Lutheran Church in the South to prepare by-laws for its government, in drafting such by-laws, so to formulate them as to require every teacher or professor who may be appointed as a teacher or professor in any Theological Seminary she may establish or put into operation, to take an obligation not to teach, practice or inculcate anything that comes in conflict with these principles, or the doctrines of the Church."

Accordingly, in 1887 at Savannah, the Rev. Dr. Socrates Henkel reported the following by-law, which was printed in the Minutes and laid over until the next meeting, at which it was again postponed:

"Every minister, teacher, professor, or missionary, in any institution or enterprise under the supervision or control of this United Synod, before entering on the performance of the duties of his office, shall make an affirmation that he will inculcate nothing that is in conflict with the Doctrinal Basis of this United Synod as defined in its Constitution, but that all his religious teachings shall be in conformity with the same; and that he will not foster nor encourage intercommunion or altar-fellowship with non-Lutherans, or unionistic services, or any secret society of a doubtful or deistic character."

The introduction of this question has caused great unrest. On the one hand the Tennessee Synod in 1888 repeated the resolutions of 1886 and threatened to withhold its coöperation until the by-law is adopted. It holds that it is not its intention to force its position on the other Synods, but simply to protect itself. It cannot conscientiously assist in any general undertaking which does not acknowledge these principles. On the other hand, some have interpreted these "four points" as an attempt to commit the whole United Synod to what is called "Close Communion" and complete separation from all other Christian people, and this is held to be a denial that Christians not of the

Lutheran Faith are of the Christian Church and within the pale of salvation. The North Carolina Synod has made its coöperation to depend on the excision of the last clause of the by-law. No doubt, the question has been shifted, and many are put into a serious dilemma; for while they disapprove of "promiscuous communion," and exchange of pulpits, and of "secret societies of a doubtful or deistic character," they are far from unchurching those of more or less divergent faith. The questions involved have never been fully discussed, and the churches in the South are not prepared to set forth their final answer; and therefore either an adoption or a summary rejection of this By-law cannot but prove a serious disaster to all of them.

Accordingly, at Knoxville, in 1892, the United Synod declared its persuasion that it was not able to express a unanimous judgment on these regulations, and simply adopted the By-laws without the proposed regulations relative to the common work of the Synods. The purport of this action is to leave the question undecided, and to recognize the difference of opinion which exists.

The efficiency, and perhaps the continued existence of the United Synod, seems to depend on the establishment of a central Theological Seminary, which, in expounding the doctrines of the Church, may not be too greatly moved by the questions which agitate the General Bodies in the North.

The Constitution of a Theological Seminary has been adopted (1892); its Board of Directors has been organized; the Seminary at Newberry has been recognized as the Seminary of the United Synod; and Rev. A. C. Voigt has been elected professor of Theology.

The means of the Southern Churches are strained to the utmost to take possession of every point of vantage in their rapidly developing territory. But it is to be hoped that nothing may interrupt this union of all the Lutherans of this section in one Confession of faith and one mode of worship.

www.ingramcontent.com/pod-product-compliance
Lightning Source LLC
Chambersburg PA
CBHW032135160426
43197CB00008B/646